2013
ORACLE

2013
ORACLE

Ancient Keys to the 2012 Awakening

DAVID CARSON & NINA SAMMONS

ART
GIGI BORRI

**COUNCIL
OAK BOOKS**

SAN FRANCISCO & TULSA

Council Oak Books, LLC
counciloakbooks.com

First edition. First printing.

Illustrated by Gigi Borri
Text, book and cover design by Carl Brune
Cover, card and cenote art by Gigi Borri

The Publishers gratefully acknowledge Michiel Berger and
his Maya Astronomy Page(http://www.astro.uva.nl/michielb/
maya/astro.html) for information about and drawings of the
Mayan numbers.

The authors gratefully acknowledge Joseph Rael, and especially
his book *The Way of Inspiration* (Tulsa: Council Oak Books),
for background information regarding Native American
numerology.

Printed in China

ISBN-13: 978-1-57178-194-9
(ISBN-10: 1-57178-194-3)

In memory of
Dr. Gabriel Slonina Ubaldini
of Urbino, Italy.

CONTENTS

THIRTEEN COUNT CARDS

ACKNOWLEDGMENTS

The authors are grateful to the holy people who we have known, practitioners of Canadian and American sundances and Mesoamerican sun ceremonies and dances. Thank you for your sharing, grace and teachings. We are particularly thankful to the great writer, scholar and midwife of of Native American Studies, Paula Gunn Allen. Thank you, Paula, for the inspiration and for the magic you have brought to our lives. With utmost respect to two other great writers and friends, Carlos Castanada and Frank Waters--gone perhaps but never forgotten and we say thank you.

Gratitude to our respective families and especially to Elizabeth, Margaret, Sara and Greta who have all contributed to the work with encouragement and insightful comments. Thanks to Mr. B. OK, Fred Sammons.

For our friends living in the green hills of Parma, Italy, Barbara Lombati and Suzanna Corrodi. Our love to Barbara Ubaldini and her family.

Special acknowledgement and thanks to Gershon Winkler, Lakme Batya Elior and the late Bob Levin, the spirit of Walkingstick Foundation. We are indebted to Gabriel Morgan for his inspiring and unflagging enthusiasm for the written word. Thanks are due to our dear friend, astrologer Rhonda Flemming. Your star messages have proven to be infallible predictions.

Thanks to Louise Rubin for coffee magic and water lily medicine. And thanks to our indefatigable agent Gary Heidt at Imprint Agency. Many thanks are due to our publisher and editor Dr. Sally Dennison at Council Oak Books. With admiration, we thank you for taking an unruly manuscript, seeing its merit, and transforming it into this present work.

DAVID CARSON & NINA SAMMONS

THE COSMIC SERPENT

Consider all of unrecorded time.

Imagine early twilight in the ancient world. Showers of brilliant cloud-stars are flung like jewels across the heavens. Now imagine the sound of your footsteps as you approach the crest of a hill. There is a crackling of energy in the air like the afterlife of the blows of a thousand lightning strikes.

Suddenly, you are overcome with fear. Your senses sharpen. A dark shape holds your consciousness, narrows your focus and your awareness. You know that this could be the magic serpent that only the great initiates confront. You have prayed, sacrificed, fasted and searched the world over to face the power and teachings of the boned white one—the cosmic serpent.

Now your quest is over. You have brought yourself before the fantastic being. Stars are mirrored in its unblinking eyes. You scan the night sky, confirming the snake's long body lies parallel to the dark knife severing our galaxy. And you feel a hot and sweet-smelling breath enveloping you. The enormous fanged mouth opens and you feel yourself pulled toward it—closer, closer. You are quickly swallowed. You hear howling winds and strange, angry voices pulling you inward. The tiniest light appears and you are hurled through blackness toward it.

Then you are walking on that dark path between the stars.

Long before the people of fifteenth-century Europe landed their boats on this continent called Turtle Island, there were realized teachers walking this sacred land. Indeed, these teachers knew a depth of metaphysics more sophisticated than anywhere else on earth. Their teachings were unheeded by the colonizers. The knowledge was covered over and removed from historical records. Much of it was sent up in smoke. The great Venus-Sun Calendar of the ancient astronomers predicts with mathematical certainty that on December 22, 2012, a new ray of creation will stream into our planetary system.

Our motherworld will be completely reborn and literally shifted into a new world.

Where the ancient teachers came from is not clear. Some said they came in wind-driven canoes. Others maintained they came from distant stars. Still others argued that they came from unknown futures. Many legends are told that these self-realized and learned ancients merged with true light when they departed. The old ones went into another dimension of existence. The science of contemplating life with an eye trained on the heavens was withdrawn into the shadows as Turtle Island came under siege by the invaders.

2013 Oracle draws upon teachings from these empires of American mound-building cultures and the Mesoamerican temple builders. Temple and earth temple complexes stretched from northern Canada to Peru. Ancient seers knew that temples contained a double, the male temple in the sky and the female temple inside the earth. The temple in the earth circulated energy along gridlines. The male sky temple recorded cosmic history. The structure and form of these monuments corresponded to the entire universe. Sky temples manifested a numinous strand that linked with all other activated temples. The strands were not lines as we experience them but inter-dimensional connections. Any point on the strand contained information on the symmetry of the entire temple complex. In other words, Spiro Mound in Oklahoma connected energetically to the spiritually charged Inka city of Qospo. The knowledge kept by these ancient temple priests and priestesses has been a mystery to modern people who share western consensus beliefs. However, this is the time of revelation and the time of the return of the prophets.

Myths abound. A variety of enigmatic stories have been passed down, encoding the creation of life and describing the forces that enliven this plane of existence. Cultures of the Americas and Mesoamerica left a legacy of cryptoprophetic information for us to ponder and study. They left accurate prophecies hidden in sacred mathematics and calendarical schemata. Most of the prophecies have already come to pass.

The prophecies agree that we are nearing the close of this world.

Some say we are at the end of the Piscean age and the beginning of the Age of Aquarius. Some call it the end of the great Kali Yuga. Others claim it to be the end of the nine hells. There is a question as to whether we are at the beginning of the Fifth, Sixth or Seventh Sun. This shift is called the New Humanity, a new creation. It doesn't matter the name we give the next sun or world. Prophecy says this is a time of transition to a new cycle of existence.

The 2013 Oracle is woven from the threads of light we call time. On or about winter solstice 2012, our Sun transits across our galactic center, a place known to the ancients as the Great Serpent or the Dark Womb of the Milky Way Galaxy. Modern astronomers call it the black hole, a place from which new stars are continually being born and old ones are continually being destroyed. When our Sun crosses into this new hemisphere, a new light moves into our solar system, the cosmic clock turns over like an odometer and begins anew. A new time sequence called New Sun or New Humanity is born from the threads of this new light.

CHARTING THE GALACTIC SEAS

Ancient people saw the designs and left knowledge for us. The basic building units used were the circle or zero, the point, the line, the square and the triangle. From chaos, these basic shapes generated harmony, beauty and order. Ultimately, humanity entered a new cycle of cosmic discernment. Celestial constructs were used as levers to elevate consciousness.

Point is a cosmic punctuation mark—the great oneness reduced and sharpened to a single increment. Mathematically, point is a microcosm. Two points joined together generate a line. Square and rectangle are male and are composed of right angles. The square, like a brick, is both social and rigid and more fixed in space than a circle. The square traps energy whereas the circle liberates it.

Triangles are a base three, and govern and unite matter and its offspring. Triangles balance positive and negative force in order to enhance the creative principle. Triangles are born of time and are a conceptual step to the understanding of the fourth dimension, since the fourth dimension is of itself an acceleration of time.

Dimensions overlap, one with another, and exist within temporal paradigms. The ancients understood the true measure of time more deeply than any modern culture. Time is a living entity. Waves of time have personality and possibility. 2013 Oracle marries sacred information with a divination system that mirrors our internal and eternal truth. The voice of the Oracle leads us through the contradictions we are facing. The ancient timekeepers have cast long shadows into our lives.

Long ago, bundles containing cycles of time were opened by the gods and measure flooded the universe. Many generations of priest and priestess mathematicians and astronomers labored to understand the form and character of time. By careful observation, these ancient scientists constructed brilliant calendars that have never since been equaled. Numbers are imbued with unseen powers. Over the centuries, the numerical values thirteen and twenty were brought forward as highly significant and became a sacred pair based on the subtle energies of our place in the universe. These numbers have been central to many divination systems.

As so often happened, the discernment and use of this sacred geometry and sequencing was guarded and cloaked in animal symbols so as not to be misused or profaned. For example, the ancestors wove the teachings of the jaguars so we could plainly see the face of the sun in each representation. Jaguar's heart is a vessel that holds Venus, Earth and Moon. The beating of the celestial heart creates the vibratory fusion of fate, chance and synchronicity, unveiling meaning. Jaguar represents the sacred number twenty. Earth and heaven unite in twenty. The *tzolk'in* calendar is a day count consisting of two intermeshing gears or wheels, one gear bears thirteen numbers and the other gear bears twenty signs. Working simultaneously they revolve and measure out a unit of time that is two hundred sixty days. This is the divinatory calendar and the period of human gestation. Tzolk'in means sacred day count, pieces of the sun and vibrational tree consciousness. Trees are the planetary breath gate. The mound and temple builders say, "Human lives are really the lives of trees."

Thirteen is the magical number of Plumed Serpent ascending into the thirteen heavens. The mystical snake courses through the universe animating all of life with its power. This holy energy is responsible for creation and destruction in micro- and macrocosm. The living force known as *k'ul* is indestructible. The wavelike body of the snake pulses through all of matter. Time is a constant. But what happens energetically and quickly in the span of a second also happens gradually over the span of a century. Both a second in time and a century have a similar sequencing but the frequencies change.

Each number in the Thirteen Count and each depiction of the imagery of the Twenty Count is utilized not only for revelatory significance but also to evoke power. Each number is infused with aspects of a cosmography of ancient teachings. The Twenty count represents the deconstruction of old values and the realization of heightened human potential. Thirteen represents spirit—that quality which continues over time.

Humanity exists as if it were blind. With the arrival of new fields of light or waveforms, our situation will completely change. The year 2013, twenty and thirteen united, ushers in the dawn of the New Humanity. Late in the year 2012 this unique spectrum will build to an unprecedented intensity. The deep structures of matter glimpsed only by the great initiates will be available to all. The shift of light will greatly enhance prophetic and visionary ability, an all-pervasive clarity born from the light of a New Sun. Mystical states and revelations will be available to all people and not just a privileged few. The prophecies never spoke of finality or endings; rather they spoke of cyclic completion. The prophecies spoke of a leap in spiritual understanding, the dissolving of limitations and the birth of a New Humanity.

The 2013 Oracle is a guide, a preview of that New Sun, bringing revelations and clarity as it unfolds the cosmic patterning underlying any life situation. Use it to enter the new, post-2012 Mind.

A PROGRESSION OF NEW LIGHT

The coming world will be as different from our current one as day is from night. This world belongs to the black magicians who will destroy it, according to some prophetic scenarios—with greed, avarice and a lust for power. Late in the year 2012, manufactured time will end. There will be a complete shattering of the dark mirrors of time's illusion, revealing dimensions that will sustain and nourish us. New light will be born and humanity will stand in this new light. We cannot predict the exact nature of the coming world, because it is beyond any known principles we can use as guides.

This great turning to the next Sun will herald an evolutionary bounce. Humanity may take a step, opening the pineal gland, enabling us to employ our full paranormal powers. Humans can become cosmic antennas in tune with the myriad territories of the Great Mind. The third eye will open for the responsive inhabitants of the entire planet, creating a world of saints, avatars and realized magicians.

We are grateful to the ancients who sent their prayers for future generations skyward on clouds of sacred tobacco smoke. In the closing of this round, Creator Himself/Herself is opening His/Her tobacco pouch to pray into existence the revelation of the new dimensions.

Remember, the old ones did not desert humanity. Master geometricians and metaphysicians left descriptions of these dimensional shifts to help future generations. These learned ones understood that the evolution of the human was incomplete and that our species faced great wars, natural catastrophes and other hardships before humanity developed the consciousness to enter the New Creation.

During our own historical interval, we witness many changes. They are accelerating and they will be swift, shocking and complete. The prophecies are explicit and horrifying. If humanity continues to pollute the earth and destroy the ecosystems that support life, polar icecaps will melt. The planet will shift in rotational axis. There will be massive earthquakes accelerated by sunspots and other celestial activity. Be assured, however, no prophet has authoritatively forecast a time when humanity has no choice in its ultimate destiny. Each one of us is responsible for a positive outcome for the transition we are seeing.

2013 Oracle is the ancient map left by the ancestors to help us make a leap into infinite possibility. Our ancestors left us a compendium of knowledge because they saw their descendents would face turbulent times. They studied the heavens and charted the changing stars and their wisdom was recorded. They penetrated the dynamic cosmos and saw how the future would unfold. They applied this knowledge to harmonizing life on earth with the heavens. The knowledge was sculpted into stone and clay and laid out in the design of the cities and calendars. It was hidden within ritual and sacrifice.

THE 2013 ORACLE CARDS

The symbols on the cards are celestial and terrestrial and can be used in many modes of meditation, dreaming, and creative visualization. At the beginning of each New Moon, select one card from the Thirteen Count Cards to help choose the path for that particular Moon Cycle. Hold the energy of the card and think of it as a biorhythmic synchronizer that opens and develops spiritual potential on your monthly journey. Also, pay attention to your dreaming during this period and let the process extend your awareness and give you nudges in the right direction.

The cards can help us climb the inter-dimensional stairway to clearer understanding of our own times and of the shift to be completed in the near future. The teeth of the divination gears turn throughout the 2013 Oracle. The system holds the teachings encoded in earth mounds, observatories, the principles that inform the Kukulkan temple at Chichen Itza and the sacred Ball Court at Monte Alban. This knowledge is hidden in the glyphs of stelae and objects of jade and bone. Sacred information is encoded in mounds and story belts, celebrations and sacred dances. The 2013 Oracle is an invitation to find the spirit in spirit and form within form. At its center is the possibility of escape and emancipation from the prison of materialism and rote existence.

There are thirty-four 2013 Oracle Cards. Every 2013 Oracle Card is described, and its divinatory meaning is revealed in the following pages. The prophetic wisdom awaits you.

TWENTY COUNT CARDS

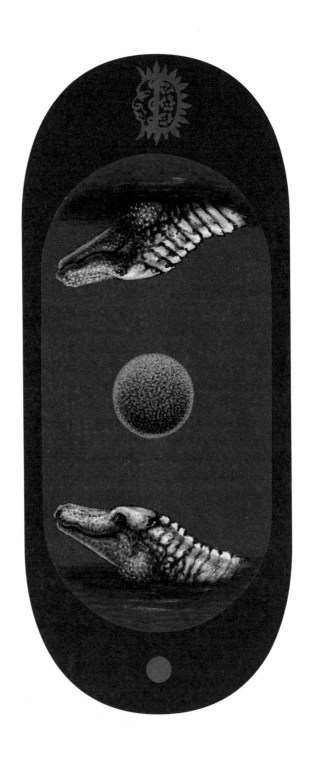

ONE

●

ALLIGATOR
Regeneration of Worlds

Teachers of old were often asked, "What will the next world be like?"

The old seers answered, "When the next world comes it will be like an Alligator. Alligator lies buried in the water and mud near the bank, never stirring. So it seems. Yet without warning, Alligator will leap out of the water and seize you. Screaming and struggling to no avail, Alligator will plunge you deep into the river and spirit you away. It will come like that."

There is a story about Alligator. Long ago in the world before we humans peopled the earth, the stars and planets were not stable. This was because Bead Spitter God had a mouth full of beads. He was monstrous-looking and a fearsome god to be reckoned with. Bead Spitter God rolled a bead onto his tongue and spit it at a star or planet. When the bead hit, it either exploded the star in fantastic light showers or caused it to streak across the heavens. This entertained Bead Spitter God to no end. This is how Bead Spitter God amused himself before we measured time, long before days and nights.

At any rate, the sleeping Alligator God, who was submerged deep in the void, became annoyed with the fiery conflagrations and continual disturbances. She asked politely for Bead Spitter to knock it off. Bead Spitter let a bead fly and it hit Alligator in the nose with a stinging smack. Alligator charged across the great emptiness while Bead Spitter headed for a distant world. Alligator soon overtook him and bit Bead Spitter on the leg. Bead Spitter fell on Alligator. Locked in immortal combat, they rolled across the heavens. Alligator emerged

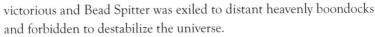

victorious and Bead Spitter was exiled to distant heavenly boondocks and forbidden to destabilize the universe.

Alligator went back and submerged herself in the mud at the center of our galaxy. Over time, the mud that collected on her back became the First World. Earth floats in a pool of stars on Alligator's back. Alligator is in communication with the Sun who calls her to reawaken and bring a new world into being. She has birthed many Worlds. Elders tell us that Alligator is awakening from her slumbers to seek the food of a new creation. She is sensitive to the waters of change and moves to bring about the regeneration of worlds

Alligator is the watcher. She glides between two worlds to the beat of her four-chambered heart, slowly–slowly. Her heart is the song-beat of the dawning of a new time. She is our guide. She prepares the way for us to meet the sudden changes, which are upon us.

Alligator was the first mound builder. Her mounds, surrounded by water, form the continents of Earth. Humans live upon the mounds that Alligator shaped. In the night sky, Alligator is a group of watcher stars called the Little Dipper. She swims about in the world below while we are asleep. Alligator is the ancient keeper of the inner spheres, the old one who holds the memories of lost ages. She can return to the past when time was different. On her journey, she passes through many spiritual realms.

Alligator tells you to find the medicine waters of life. There are Alligator mounds in Louisiana near the shores of Grand Lake. These mounds were put there to remind us of the coming of Alligator's spirit and the emerging New Earth and New Humanity. After Alligator's awakening, waters of chaos will be calmed, smoothed, cleared and evened. Alligator is a predator and is the guardian of doors. In her mouth are worlds, universes, different levels of reality and spirit. According to the prophecy of the mound builders, alligator, snake and other mounds will be activated by Venus. Meridians will be energized along the spine of the Earth. The mounds will be used in ceremony and it is through ceremony that the Earth will completely awaken. Alligator's mouth will open hastening the onset of humanity's healing. The prophets, seers and diviners will return. What has been sealed shut, opened.

The hidden will be found. What is whispered will be shouted. All prophecy of our creation will be revealed and completed.

Alligator teaches us respect for elders and this card suggests you spend some time with older men or women. Mine their experience and spiritual understanding. See to the comfort of the elderly and provide for them. Elders may be in jeopardy or peril. Their health may be compromised. If this is true, Alligator asks you to remedy the situation.

Use this card to awaken from your dreams and fantasies and shrewdly pursue your cravings and desires. Be bold. Be rash. The sentinel Alligator sees deeply into the muddy waters preventing our clarity. She sees the infinite dimensions of this universe. She sees the destiny of this world. Seek to open your own water-smoked eyes and see beyond the river. Find the truth behind the truth. See through the murky swamp vapors and the mud and once you see your opportunity, seize it. Be daring.

COSMIC WHIRLWIND
Androgyny

An understanding of Cosmic Whirlwind gives us a map for navigation through life's turnings. Through swirls of night and day, we are driven. Cosmic Whirlwind has the power to roll us around endlessly like marbles. We are but play toys in the shifting whirlpools of fate.

Cosmic Whirlwind contains both male and female energies, and is keeper of the spirit of a third power—the energy of Androgyny. In our entire universe there are only these three powers—male, female and androgynous. By living consciously and finding the precious fulcrum, one can manifest enormous control of energy—the power of the Whirlwind. Cosmic Whirlwind is many things. Cosmic Whirlwind is the conch shell and the wind jewel. It is the human heart offered in sacrifice, and sacrifice spirals us to the new consciousness of 2013.

Cosmic Whirlwind is associated with Venus and symbolized by Snail. The temples of Venus contained a mysterious geometry that was perfectly aligned with the movement of this planet. Stairways in the ancient Mesoamerican Venus observatories are spiraled like a snail, curving around and around. At the center of Whirlwind is a secret reversing eye, drawing you into utter stillness.

Cosmic Whirlwind figures deeply in the creation of matter and teaches us about the double spiral. Just as with the rotations of Earth and Venus, one spiral goes clockwise and the other spiral goes counterclockwise. This geomagnetic energy leaves its imprint on life-forming DNA. Snail is a gate to the spiraling inner world of spirit. She is keeper of the whirlwinds of masculine and feminine powers.

We seek the imperishable and the eternal. There is no such thing as sexual difference in the spirit world. When gender identification

is dissolved, the human can make a connecting link between the self and all. As we spiral through the whirlpools of life, we can find liberty and freedom from the confines of the paradoxes of sexuality. By respecting the essential right of all beings to exist, we can mold a new consciousness. We can set a course for a world where all life forms are elevated and venerated. Whirlwind teaches you to make choices. That is the real lesson of androgyny. This teaching isn't about plus or minus. It is where the scales balance. Androgyny is neutral and, just as in an automobile, neutral is an important gear.

In order to survive this incarnation on our shrinking planet, we must learn to live in harmony and peace with one another. We must get along with each other in a world that seems bent on hating and destructive behaviors. Whirlwind says to recognize the paradoxes of identity.

If Whirlwind has appeared in your cards today, find a place of balance and then make balanced decisions. Power is with you. Cosmic Whirlwind brings zest, new vitality and youthful beauty. Now is the time to spin your medicine, charge in and start a project or finish one. If a certain situation has come to a standstill, put it on hold until you can arrive at the objectivity you need to make further progress.

We have chosen to manifest at this time, in this body, and in our present social and political milieu. Before we incarnated, we were pure androgynous spirit. This spirit became a whirlwind. Revolving, spiraling, our soul waited to find a mother and father who would meet our needs. Upon conception, we received our sexual identity. Yet always, deep in our psyches, we remember our former spiritual state and we long to return to this pure essence.

Seeking sanctuary, the mystic cries out to Creation—to the Great One at the center of the Milky Way and to the portal of all that lies beyond. Ancestors and other spirit beings emerge from this mouth to communicate with the human visionary. The heart is at the center of our beloved galaxy where we must face our challenge to live in harmony with the cosmos. Creation holds us with compassion and no judgment.

You climb upwards on the winding stairs of life in the footfalls of those who came before you. The stairs begin at birth and end at death. There is a banister to cling to as you climb or stumble. The banister consists of your beliefs, culture, race, religion, family, relationships, sexual orientation, ego and profession. The banister is your ignorance or your bliss. As you follow the course of your life, changes appear as you round each bend, for always the banister turns.

Cosmic Whirlwind Card presages erratic turns in the lives of rulers, presidents, people in positions of authority and even the lowliest of bureaucrats. Popularity may plummet. This may bring uncertainty to the population at large. Rulers will be helpless to govern because the cosmic forces that govern them are exerting such powerful influences. Confusing and unstable economic conditions may prevail.

Cosmic Whirlwind asks you to watch out for the toxins in your life. Perhaps do some fasting or cleansing. Be conscious of the food you eat. Make sure it is pure and life-sustaining. Do whatever you can to protect the environment—the land, the water and the air you breathe. Donate some time and energy to environmental causes so that future generations can profit from your work. If you cannot do that, at least recycle.

Your own life may be turning, spinning like a top and swaying topsy-turvy this way and that. Find your center of gravity and be still within this necessary ascension. Find a weave of rhythm with each new turn and follow the coil of your destiny. Bring your courage to a head as the past swirls away and other pressing challenges appear. Just as the earth is changing, you are also. Make choices and enjoy the scenery around the bend. The dynamic forces of Cosmic Whirlwind are releasing personal energy to a cellular level, bringing a profound new equilibrium into your surroundings. Cosmic Whirlwind is often a very favorable omen.

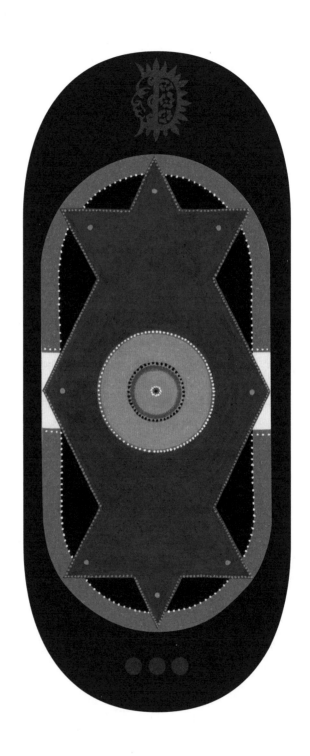

● ● ●

SACRED PRECINCT
Divine Center

Sacred Precinct is a holy place that acts as a lens to enlarge our understanding of the sacred. Sacred Precinct is connected with sacred rituals and is a spiritual manifestation of great magnitude. Sacred Precinct teaches that the Earth is a sphere, and no matter where we are, we are at center. The entire universe comes to rest in this tiny spot and is present within it. Sacred Precinct is a powerful and universal geometrical form. It has been a paradigm for religious thought throughout the ages.

The drawing of this card addresses the need for a beautiful, protected and devotional space—a nurturing place for meditation and reflection. Sacred Precinct is a powerful gate to pass through for initiation. In it is a universe where Spiritual Earth and Spiritual Sky are joined. Each sacred space is unique. Each sacred circle embodies the principles of every other sacred circle. Sacred Precinct teaches that the small is related to the totality of life and all our relatives. Ultimately, a sacred part of the totality of life resides within us.

Sacred Precinct is the sacred space that welcomes the divine center. Space is the first manifestation. Even when you imagine nothing exists, there is still space. Each place in creation is at the center of great and small. Center is the axis of great power. Sacred Precinct keeps the point of union and transformation, the point where all things are related. The entire universe comes to rest in this tiny spot, and is present within you and manifests through you. Sacred Precinct is related to all other Sacred Precincts and is not owned by any one

T
W
E
N
T
Y

C
O
U
N
T

C
A
R
D
S

religion or sect. When a sacred space is profaned or desecrated, this insult reverberates through the cosmos.

Healing is at the core of Sacred Precinct. A feature in various Sacred Precincts in ancient communities was a complex of stone sweat houses located in the center of the city. This complex of baths was known as the House of Flowers dedicated to the Eater of Filth, the healing goddess. Her image was carved over the entrance. Inside, a firebox was heated and water was poured over the top. Steam cascaded through the house.

Pregnant women, recent mothers and the sick went there to be cleansed. Copal was burned as an offering. Rituals were done to facilitate healing. As part of the healing, the patients were coated in medicinal black clay. The patient was sweated. Coming out of the sweat hut was a new birth, a new start on the healing road. Priests and priestesses struck the body with herbs and curing switches. Midwives massaged recent mothers to health and recovery.

To be in sacred space is to have personal power and it means to be in accord with your totality of being in the immediate moment. It means to be in the right place at the right time—and to know it. Sacred Precinct is a creation of the order of the universe, out of time and even out of space. Sacred Precinct teaches of the measureless delight of the measureless moment. Sacred Precinct is a great teacher that shows us the way home.

If you have drawn the Sacred Precinct Card you are being asked to remember that circle of self, your own personal life and your meaning in it. You are being asked to remember the undying love of the Great Mysterious Power that also resides in your circle. Remember that your larger self contains the whole universe. When you remember this, you will be given your divine center. Sacred Precinct asks you to look at those closest to you with new awareness. Bring sacredness into your personal sphere of influence. Walk under the canopy of creation in health and happiness.

You might want to look at your home, domicile or apartment—

even your work place—and bring spirituality and beauty into it. Put forward good energy to your environment and it will come back to you magnified. Construct a gorgeous precinct within. Apply this to the structure of your entire life. Bring the unity of the elements and let sunshine, starlight and moonglow bathe you in an increase of inner harmony. Your inner work will reflect back into your present environment. No matter where you are, Sacred Precinct Card graciously says, "Make yourself at home."

T
W
E
N
T
Y

C
O
U
N
T

C
A
R
D
S

24

●●●●

CELESTIAL TOAD
Guardian of Spirit

Celestial Toad has powers to play with conceptual thought-waves and other designs of cognition. She is regarded with awe. She is wise and sees the sacred in all things. The temple priests and priestesses are vomited from the mouth of the great Toad. She wears the yellow-spotted coat of the Jaguar. This means that she has brought the sacrament of transcendent consciousness.

When seeking to treat the imbalances and spiritual maladies that lead to mental unease and disease, there is no better power to call upon than Celestial Toad. Celestial Toad sends protection to spiritual seekers and lights the way to spiritual truth. She is in the night sky and renews our life as part of the night-day cycle. She is the one with feathered knives from above. She is found as a constelaetion of stars. She awakens in the silence and in the darkness. Your acceptance of Celestial Toad takes you into a world of no boundaries. Celestial Toad is often called the "birth canal," meaning that she births you to a heightened state of awareness.

Celestial Toad is an excellent diviner and has the power to isolate and transform danger when it is near. She is the power by your left side. Celestial Toad can warn of earthquakes, meteor strikes or other natural disasters. Forewarned is forearmed. She is the keeper of many secret disciplines and is a mistress of many lost energetic realms. She is associated with healing at a distance. She is the mistress of the subtle use of various kinds of bewitching animal and plant substances.

There are massive Toad altars and there are stelae-carvings that show the Toad with exaggerated glands behind her head. In these

●●●●

depictions, scrolls swirl out of the body. This denotes a non-ordinary state. This giant Toad produces a powerful hallucinogen known as *bufotenine* through these large glands.

Temple Priests harvested a white juice from these Toads. This was done by holding them tightly while searing the creature between the eyes with the glowing tip of a hot stick. The juice that was then freed from Toad was scraped from the glands. It was gathered at the dark of the moon. These powerful psycho-chemicals were mixed with pulverized tobacco. The vision-producing snuff was then inhaled and this was an accelerated monorail ride to other dimensions. It was a shotgun blast across time to the locus of the God principle. The beings of this new territory often presented the voyager with gifts. One might see into the future or be cured of a disease. However, an encounter with the lords or ladies of this otherworld was not always pleasant. Information obtained in this manner might reveal painful truths.

Look to this card to help you express latent powers before they become dormant and are never again capable of being used. Celestial Toad tells you to use them or lose them. This card offers you a new world of opportunity and hidden energetic capabilities. Follow these newly awakened powers, but keep silent when you go for it.

Nurturing is in the cards. Celestial Toad may bring out your mothering instincts, no matter if you are female or male. Communion with Celestial Toad has the power to sharpen creative vision. You do not have to sell out to dark powers. You can walk the earth roads in balance with light and dark. One must reckon with Toad's life force. Toad is heavily associated with the ball game and ball courts. The Toad Card may help you see how to deal with the competition. Her guidance can be useful in both physical and spiritual realms.

Celestial Toad always tells you to hop to it.

HORNED SNAKE
Precious Jewel

Horned Snake carries the energy of the fifth day of divination and follows the path of the Cosmic Serpent, Draco. There is an ancient story that tells of the mysterious powers of Horned Snake. About eight thousand seven hundred years ago the earth became enshrouded in darkness. This lasted for many years. Then the Horned Snake approached with its brilliant crown jewel illuminating the entire world around. The people saw this great light of many colors and it warmed them and filled them with joy. Such a jewel and such a light had never been seen or known to exist.

Some evil ones thought to steal the power of the precious jewel. They approached the great Horned Serpent with long knives and spears. They struck many times and the wondrous being soon writhed its last. Then they reached for the great crystal horn, and as they were removing it, it exploded. Little pieces of the light went into everything. Now it is said we must look carefully when we are searching for the precious jewel. The sages teach that a small piece of the precious jewel is inside of each being, although it is often difficult to discern.

This precious jewel now lives hidden in the rainbow. It floods all of creation with brightness but we have to learn to see it. Horned Snake teaches that within you is this miraculous light. This light not only lights your way, it can light the way for others. It is the shining jewel of friendship, love, and the warmth of kindness.

The crown jewel links Horned Snake with the upper world and to the highest purpose. Horned Snake is keeper of secret knowledge and carries the sacred fire of life. She holds light and understands and

communicates with it. Light only gives light. Horned Snake swims deep in the unconscious of us all seeking to ignite us and warm us with her sacred fires. Horned Snake is the precious one, the jeweled one who carries the code of our life's mission.

Horned Snake's horn is a powerful crystal antenna that is highly valued in the practice of healing and other related arts. The horn is able to greatly amplify good and evil. Venus is often called the mystical jewel of the morning and evening sky and can be used to activate the powers of the crystal horn of Horned Snake.

The surface of Mother Earth is two-thirds water. Horned Snake is the protector of water—of oceans, seas, lakes, rivers and streams. She guards the entrance to many worlds. She can be contacted by passing through portals, caves, cenotes and rivers. Her body mass is a powerful sequence of muscles hung on a segmented skeleton. When activated, her tail is whip-like and projects tremendous energy. When she stirs the surface of placid waters, they become unpredictable and life-threatening.

With her snake family she holds and guards the water world. The earth's crust is supported by four horned snakes. They interlock at the four directions where they provide stability. Altars may be built to honor Horned Snake and to invoke the energetic principles of water. Draw a medicine wheel with a serpent shape in each direction radiating downward as if driven into the earth like stakes.

Let Horned Snake lead you to a mystical river, which flows into deep creative powers. She blesses us with creative fluidity. Her waters are charged with energy. She is the holy intercessor swimming between shadow and light or between consciousness and the hidden depths of the unconscious. She has arrived to fill you with inspiration. Let her do just that. Horned Snake can lead you to important knowledge that you have been seeking but which has thus far eluded you. She is an omen of good fortune. Horned Snake reminds you that you are a precious jewel. You can light the world around you and make it a better place.

Horned Snake Card brings water to the seeds of your creative ideas. *The magic serpent brings the jewels of good health and sudden material gain. Jewels are created from snake saliva. Gems are the scattered celestial dust of Venus. Jewels are symbolic of wisdom grown deep within the dark earth. See the jewels all around you. Jewels represent knowledge of self, won from the unconscious. Their divine energy aligns with spiritual illumination. Jewels can heal and protect. Horned Snake, the brilliant visionary, is a serene teacher. Vision is born when you discover your inner piece of the shattered rainbow jewel. And indeed, true vision is always a Precious Jewel.*

BEE
Apprenticeship

A white flower blooms in a magic garden. This lovely white flower is the heart of the human soul. Bee is associated with mystery schools and sovereign matriarchal communal groups. The diving Bee is often symbolized by Venus. Because the virgin worker Bees construct hexagrams when building the honeycomb, the magic value of six has been linked to them. Bees work tirelessly for the good of all. They know their life path is for a noble purpose.

Bee understands various innate properties of sacred geometry and uses the wisdom in remarkable ways. This great mathmatizer uses sacred geometry in flight patterns and in the creation of the honeycomb. Bee is an inspired worker and symbolizes the search for spiritual sweetness. Bee seeks the fragrant flowers just as apprentices seek spiritual truth. Long ago, before a person became an apprentice to any spiritual system, she or he was taught to first hold council with the Bees. We listen and learn their buzzing mantra. We listen to what they have to tell us about the apprentice path. If Bee's counsel is yes, deep within you will awaken a sweet sound like the sound Bee makes. It is a joyful sound and our lips, our heart, mind, body and soul smile.

Bee is the shamaness of the flower. Bee does her singular tasks within a multiplicity of being. Bee teaches cooperation with others and has an innate understanding of the good of the whole tribe. For this reason and others, bees embody the essence of the apprenticeship spirit. Just as an apprentice is seeking spiritual honey, the Bee is gathering and sharing sweetness in a similar manner.

Bees know well the beauty way, the beauty trails. They seek the

opened blossom, caressed by the wind. They find the little ones open to the great sun. They explore the pink petals and find the life and breath gate. Bees are the great alchemists producing the quintessential essence of sweetness. They teach an esoteric rite of passage.

Spiritual teachings have been likened to beautiful flowers in a lush meadow. The Bee follows her intuition, moving from flower to flower. So must the apprentice use her intuition in understanding the teachings. Not all flowers are sweet, however. Flowers of both good and evil bloom are all about the seeker. It takes vision, it takes character, it takes work—to come to spiritual understanding. But above all, one must listen for the higher octave of sacred sound, just as a flower hears the buzzing Bee hovering overhead. This buzzing sound and vibration heralds a total change in consciousness. It is the next step of our unfolding nature.

Secret initiation ceremonies centered on the Bee as a symbol. In the rites, unity and group mind were stressed. Bees teach us that other forms of communication exist simultaneously with our own. Bees know the rules of the geometric order of creation. They teach that within the seeker there is a conscious desire to walk an exemplary road to find spiritual wisdom.

Our world is changing. Bees and butterflies skip over the bloom. Bee asks that you find the sweet attar of the mystic rose. Apprenticeship means seeking. Apprenticeship means spiritual training. It means learning the way. You must first find the spiritual teacher within. The true spiritual teacher will lift you with kindness and love—a love that burns through the universe. The apprenticeship of the Bee is the open heart. It is the secret hidden in the flower of flowers. It is the good road to the good place—the place of the awakened self, free of ignorance.

Bee Card may be calling you to a spiritual site or gathering. Use sound and vibration in your meditation. Do you have a teaching for a friend or loved one, or a special knowledge to share? If so, share it. It is said that Bee was born from the tears of the Eagle Sun. The Bee is the priest and priestess; hence, Bee is our teacher. The Beehive is the symbol for our spiritual community. If Bee has buzzed into your reading, listen to her. She is asking, where is spiritual sweetness, where is the honeycomb? What are the spiritual flowers and where are they located in your field of being? Go now to the white flower and extract its abundant nectar.

This is the way of Bee.

DEER MAN
Compassion

The Deer Man is a night creature but related to solar energies. His antlers are a symbol of the Tree of Life. When he sheds them, it is a sign there is regeneration in the cosmos. He represents virility and ardor. He teaches us to sacrifice in order to acquire compassion. He is a symbol of swiftness and solitude. He brings messages from other planes of being.

Deer Man is a mysterious creature who is seen in deep woods or forests. He is the double-headed stag who fell from the sky. Stag medicine gives him superhuman strength. He wins every spiritual battle. He knows every chamber of the human heart. It is said that Deer Man came to earth to teach the hunter-warrior how to reverence life and how to take it. The people with these teachings went to war with Smoking Mirror who was greedy for blood and devoured human hearts. Deer Man's followers defeated Hummingbird of the Left, a dark face of Smoking Mirror.

Deer Man wore a horned snake as a belt around his waist. Horned Snake was his advisor. Deer Man is a twin of the Lord of Flayed, and as such symbolizes renewal and plenty. Deer Man has appeared many times in diverse cultures over the earth. There have been many encounters with Deer Man in Middle and North America.

Deer Man is keeper of the heart. He embodies the marriage of compassion with wisdom. He has the power to melt every conflict in life. Deer is the teacher of the magic of the heart, the animator of the hand, and balm to the tangled mind. Compassion has sweet eyes and sees the sacred beauty of all life including the beauty of self.

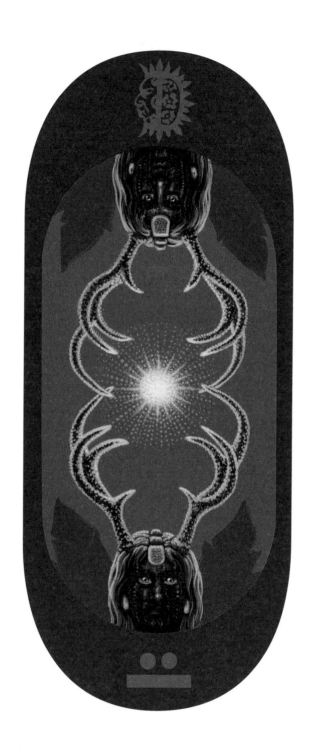

There are many old tales of meetings with Deer Man. One old tale tells of a cruel tyrant who makes life miserable for all those about him. He pillages, murders, and joyfully inflicts pain and sorrow on others. When the tyrant meets with Deer Man, he realizes his own self-loathing and fear. His heart suddenly opens and great compassion is born within him. He does his best to make amends to all he has harmed. The rest of his life is dedicated to service and loving kindness to others.

Compassion is the understanding that there are no insignificant events. A minor event affects the totality of being. When we pick up a stone or step on an insect, it very subtly changes us and our world. Our every act has meaning. Compassion seeks the highest order of perfection. Compassion is the awareness of the suffering of others. It means to help your brother or sister out of difficulty whenever you can. Compassion is the way of service. It is the greatest yes to life.

Compassion streams through the universe riding the thrumming rhythm of life. Time, space, and movement can be collapsed into one universal resonance because it is the first sound of creation—the great *Om*. Deer Man speaks a common language that links us all. Deer Man gives the power to act or not to act when confronted with problems that confound the mind.

As we search into life's mysteries, all about us we see the suffering of others. We see their struggles, their mistakes, their pain and sorrows—the deep pathos of the human condition. Compassion gives one the power of the opened heart. It is not rational, nor sentimental, nor logical—it is beyond. It is the humble strength that can move a mountain. Compassion is freedom from the material world.

Deer Man sees a world of spirits—a knowing beyond states and conditions. This means knowing purity by traveling deep into the human shadow through compassion. Compassion is the milk of experience. Compassion is courage to face and fight with yourself until you are rid of false beliefs. It is a self-compassion as well as the compassion for others. Compassion is the courage to find, acknowledge and love your true self.

Culture traps one in the game of self-importance, to strive, to get to the top. Deer Man is humble even with his great ability and strength. He knows that the intellect can be proud. He knows that true humility is one of the most difficult of all powers to carry. Deer Man knows that he doesn't know within the paradox of knowing. Compassion is beyond belief systems. It is finding your lost heart, realizing your deep love and giving it to all of creation.

If beautiful Deer Stag Man has sauntered into your card spread, open up your heart to others. Walk past fear, judgment and ego investments—your own or others. Be true to your highest light and the pulsing heart of kindness. Bring a little tenderness into your own situation or the situation of another. Bless your adversaries or at least call a truce. The sacred master deer may even show you that your enemy is your disguised friend crying out for help.

MOON GODDESS
Passages

A pearl falls from the clam shell
Rolls around inside a black bowl,
Pours down light from above
On the dark figures of women
With up-stretched arms.

Moon Goddess is draped across her throne of time, one leg hooked over the armrest. She playfully strokes her companion Rabbit held in the crook of her arm. Her headdress swirls with the numbers one through twenty-eight. She holds counsel with Monkey and a group of astronomer priests and priestesses. Monkey sits before a book with brush and inkwell. He gestures with his long skinny left arm, ink splashing from the brush as he talks excitedly.

Moon Goddess smiles indulgently.

Moon Goddess is Great Rainbow Woman and visits us night after night, month after month, year after year, until our round on earth is completed.

Meanwhile, Moon Goddess is a passionate guide for life's journeys.

Moon Goddess weaves our destiny into phases as we mark the passages of our lives. She witnesses the principal events such as conception, birth, maturity and death. She encircles us day and night. She is our constant companion and exerts irresistible influence over us. She tugs at the blood pumping through our bodies.

T
W
E
N
T
Y

C
O
U
N
T

C
A
R
D
S

Her shining face in all its aspects entwines us with her rhythm. Moon Goddess speaks to our blood and we answer. Moon Goddess speaks to the earth's blood and the watery deep answers. When we meditate on Moon Goddess, we become conscious of the water in our blood, saliva, bile, tears and sweat, and acknowledge that we are bound to her. She is our mother and we feel her in every cell of our being. We see that there is no separation.

Ancient people paid strict attention to the heavenly vault—the Sun, Moon, Venus and the stars in their courses. The beginning of solar ceremonies was plotted by the full moon. The ancients saw that the macrocosm has a direct influence on every aspect of life. This understanding has been lost. The Moon unfailingly provides humans with a series of cadences. Her body pulls on our home with such a dynamic force that we become a double planet. Yet we look uncomprehendingly at her in the sky—if we look at all.

Women who want to honor the goddess can explore the creation of a moon lodge where they can be present in a sacred space with others once a month. Men may want to address their feelings about the feminine and menstruation as an integral part of reproduction. Menses is wrapped in an uncomfortable silence in our culture. A lack of understanding and rejection of the feminine leads to a harsh dismissal of the emotional and physiological aspects of this cycle. Our greatest "magicians," the scientists, have gathered very little empirical evidence about the effects of the moon on the physical lives of women and men. But they were extremely interested in "putting a man on the moon."

Moon Goddess offered us a measure upon which we organized to become a human community and a culture. Without her, we fall into alienation and chaos. We physically deteriorate and perish. Ancient humankind was thrown into upheaval during lunar eclipses because they feared it signaled a tumultuous cosmic shift. Their observation of cosmic events had shown that interplanetary and stelaer behavior profoundly influenced life on earth. They knew that solar and lunar geomagnetic forces were mutable and ever changing.

Moon Goddess taught humans ceremonial design. Lunar passages are a ritual template. She waxes. She wanes. She disappears and is resurrected. This is one of her multifaceted gifts to humankind. The flow of the seasons on the wheel of existence and the great panorama of her faces offer us a cosmic pulse. Wrap yourself in her silvery garment of brightness.

Moon Goddess in your reading signals the need for a ritual calendar in your life. Don't be surprised to find yourself scouring texts from your tradition to create ceremony for yourself and others. Examine the deeper meaning of the holidays you keep. Is it time to reconfigure your calendar? Bring moon cycles into your daily routine. Plant and harvest accordingly. Look beyond the immediate to the power behind the scenes. Moon Goddess radiates powerful intuition. She offers you the milk of human evolution and of human kindness. Beneficent is her nature.

The Moon has promised to serve the people until the end of time. "I will be a comfort in the night and a beacon to guide you," says Moon Goddess. "I will mark your human trail with measure and beauty."

She calls to you even in the darkest night.

OBSIDIAN KNIFE
Severance

This, then, is the dark book of the beginning. The time is now and a great storm is gathering on the spiritual planes. Lightning shatters the blue-black sky like a dark egg cracking open and brilliant light comes spilling out of it. Next comes thunder. Knives clash. The icy winds blow. Wind and rain swirl in the night. Pages rustle and stir in the *Book of Days*, the ancient book of prophecies. The pages flip quickly and open to Eighth Sky. These leaves, too, are torn away, scatter and are lost in the howling wind.

Now in the Ninth Sky there are twisted people wielding twisted flint knives. Their spirits have been mutilated. Beware of these beautiful twisted ones. There are many. With convoluted speech, they will twist every situation. They will manipulate you. Stabbing with twisted knives, they will force you onto paths you were never meant to tread. They can only lead you to the land of the terrible feathered knives where they will lock you in a maze of cold and cutting flint.

But there is another kind of knife.

Black the knife. Red the cut. Obsidian the edge.

Wisdom dwells in the Land of No Flesh and Obsidian Knife teaches about the spirit world.

In fact, most religions teach of the sacrifice. The human family tells many stories holding for and against sacrificial doctrines. Wars were fought over bloodletting and ritual sacrifice. Most modern-day rituals and ceremonies have an acknowledgement of sacrifice latent within them. The ancient scholars believed that without maintaining a subtle balance of sacrifice, our world would go to ruin.

There is a true path of the knife. The Obsidian Knife blade represents shadow and the cut represents light. At the heart of this ritual object is the cutting away of illusion. Metaphysically, a severance is also a joining at this meeting place of light and shadow. On the path of the Obsidian Knife no one can carry a burden. No one can walk with you. You may bear neither left nor right. The cutting edge does not allow for mistakes. One must use this holy knife in a strict, correct, impeccable way.

The sharp edge of the blade means understanding. To stay on the path you must keep balanced. On your walk along the edge, you must place one foot before another. You must be sure to have perfect equilibrium. There cannot be the slightest error. The great initiates of the past treaded this same precarious bridge across the knife's blade.

Obsidian Knife is a drastic metaphor. Obsidian Knife speaks of realization as a form of death. When you realize a spiritual truth, you lose a lie. Your false belief is cut away. This ritual knife is used to cut away illusion. On the path of the obsidian blade one must be fully awake. All great religious traditions teach that in order to have life we must also lose it. This is the teaching of Obsidian Knife. Obsidian Knife speaks of realization as a form of death. This kind of awakening is often a very painful process.

Look at what you need to remove from your life. Drop it in Eagle Bowl and send it upward as a present to the Sun. If you have drawn Obsidian Knife Card, be careful of injurious, cutting remarks. Obsidian Knife can be a warning about some problem that should be dealt with immediately. Quit procrastinating.

Stay away from cutting people and any kind of verbal fencing. If not, you may even get stabbed in the back or have some very unpleasant exchange. The cut can be so sharp and deep you may not even realize you have been wounded. Then the pain hits and the cold, shocking, truth is realized. If you inadvertently find yourself in the House of Razors, you must cut a deal with the slicing blades. No other choice. You must promise to give the

OBSIDIAN KNIFE

blade its victim. It is either you or another because someone must pay the blade.

Let the Holy Knife show you what changes must be made. Obsidian Knife is an extension of your will to be used to restore balance following a traumatic incident. Obsidian Knife is the knife of fate and may require spiritual submission and forgiveness for those who have hurt you. It may require a new openness and vulnerability. Address your avoidance issues. Make friends with the plant people—food plants, plants of beauty, trees and medicine plants. Simplify your life and avoid excess. Spend some night hours cutting away from noise. Turn your gaze heavenward to the shimmering silence of the starry river.

Obsidian Knife Card tells you to keep appointments, especially dental appointments. Sharpen kitchen knives or scissors, your senses and your wit. Visit a barber or beauty shop. The card bodes well for minor surgery. No longer can you live in denial. Face difficult problems. First, introspect and find exactly what you need to do. Let Obsidian Knife protect you from evil or psychic attack. Use it to ward off negativity and banish powers that are inimical to you, your family or friends.

Lastly, consider this teaching of the Obsidian Knife. If you are going to use it, cut quickly and be in perfect accord with what you are doing. Once done, it cannot be undone. Thank the knife and bless it for its power. The precious knife must then be cleansed with Obsidian Knife Water, run through copal smoke, wrapped in red cloth and put away for safekeeping until needed.

WATER DOG
Metamorphosis

Water Dog, the salamander, is a beautiful creature. He tells you that you are undergoing metamorphosis and moving from one stage to the next. He can help you process pain or loss and minimize any sort of suffering. Life must evolve—adapt and re-adapt. This inner change depends entirely on you. Only you can determine the direction. But Water Dog leads you on a journey to your deepest understanding and guides you through profound shifts of consciousness. He is the master teacher of the art of metamorphosis. There is no better instructor of this lost alchemy than Water Dog.

Water Dog is the child of our closest stars and the twin brother of the Plumed Serpent. Sun was his father and Moon was his mother. Venus, his aunt, was responsible for teaching him the mystical powers of metamorphosis. Water Dog, to honor his Venusian teacher, mixes together the process of involution and evolution and transforms them into spiritual gold—the gold of wisdom. He transits from suffering to a continual state of bliss that only the highest avatars attain. He crawls into the mud and suspends his life functions, accepting whatever comes, willing himself to be changed. When the dark rains begin to fall, he emerges from his confinement vitally renewed.

Salamander's spirit can align you with the miraculous metamorphosis transpiring on the planet. Old laws of time and space are collapsing. Old structures of thought are being dismantled brick by doctrinal brick. New systems of belief are replacing old ones. Gateways to spiritual realms are thrown open. Salamander holds the alchemical

keys to alter the evil under our present Sun. Salamander has a heart of fire. He represents spiritual courage and the courage to allow his state of being to be totally reinvented. Ceremonies led by priestesses called on the magical powers of Salamander. Nine secret rites led one back into the genesis of life. Salamander, the child of the Sun and Moon, facilitated this passage. *Enlist Water Dog to help you find the elemental spark of life. With that spark, initiate the changes you need to make.*

> *Water Dog is able to bring relief to mental strains and discomfort. You may not be able to right wrongs but you will be able to tolerate them. You will be able to remix and reshape your feelings. Much of the negative impact of a given situation can be mitigated now with Water Dog's energy. Selecting Water Dog, you are given powers to protect yourself against the daily bludgeoning and shocks of our times. When you feel yourself aghast at the barbarism and harshness of human struggle, Water Dog can help you. He counsels you to take resolve and use his morphic power. He promises to rejuvenate you and restore your mental harmony. Let your quest for peace and happiness enliven your spirit. Walk the Salamander Path.*

People get locked from the inside looking out and there is no way to make necessary changes because there is no insight into the true situation. We become imprisoned by our judgments and by our false projections. We make problems and difficulties for ourselves and create enemies where none exist. We create obstacles when we think we can only behave and relate to the world according to our habituated patterns.

> *Salamander's genius is to make you know yourself, to make you see with your burst eyes what you are doing. It is not "them;" it is you. With this realization the holding pattern is over. You no longer have to accept the status quo. You must change. Find the flowing tranquil waters carrying you to your perfect spiritual metamorphoses. Make the decision to go with the flow.*

> *Water Dog knows when the waters of earth are targeted so be*

aware and keep in harmony with water. Make sure you are not dehydrated. Water stimulates dreaming and returns lost memories. Perhaps you should visit a sacred spring, waterfall or cenote. You were born of original water so let Salamander lead you back to that original reservoir. Salamander teaches that we can chant and pray over water and bring it to its pristine state.

Water Dog Card has come to help you do exactly that. Choose not to suffer. Don't make it difficult. Choose not to struggle and transition away from constraints. Water Dog asks you why you continue to be so limited in your vision when you can emerge to new levels of creative potential. To do this, you need only to be true to your unique self. Let the beautiful Salamander guide you. Go through that dark and hidden passageway to a complete metamorphosis. Salamander has come to infuse you with new life.

ELEVEN

MONKEY
Mind

Thinking about thinking about thinking about thinking about thinking.

Think about Monkey.

The Sacred Twins conned their older brothers up a ceiba tree and tricked them into becoming Monkeys. This great tree is a metaphor for the human brain—the roots, the Moon House Tree, and the branches, the Sun House Tree. The tree is analogous to the network of the mind and has been Monkey's territory ever since.

Monkey teaches nothing is out there. It is all in the mind and there is only one Mind. Mind is a great trickster that can lead us away from Great Spirit. The Mind is capricious, tells lies and plays head games, as they are called. The Mind is a chittering Monkey spoofing you in all manner of devious ways. Beware of the Mind.

Moon called and Monkey climbed up the worlds to the Eighth Heaven. The spirit of Monkey has been playing hide-go-seek with the solar and cosmic beings ever since. Monkey brought Mind, and with it unpredictability, irony and mischief-making. The Earth was perfect in every way until Monkey threw a piece of broken conch shell at it. This caused havoc with the winds and many major disruptions in Earth's harmony. Our planet has never fully recovered from this incident.

North is the place of the intellect. Monkey is associated with the direction north, and aligned astronomically with the North Star. His right hand is flailing in your face. But what secrets are in his left arm?

He gazes at Cloud Serpent and goes his Monkey-monk way guided by a different light. Like a drunken monkey, he rolls around on the ground patting his belly, chattering and chittering. He's laughing at you. He seems to be harmless enough, but he rules over weapons that strike from a distance—spears, arrows and blow darts.

Monkey Star Man, the Black Monkey of the Pole Star, the North Star, is always there to orient you and give you direction. In fact, all the stars continually dance around Black Monkey. Black Monkey claps his hands and sings a circle song while the feathered stars rotate above on the Roof of Time and dance their ritual dance. Monkey Star Man is a powerful god.

With Monkey Mind you can be playful. Monkey often gets lost in a land of delights—tasting, smelling, touching, hearing and seeing. Let your actions mirror a certain playful hedonism. Monkey swings from one sensorial branch to another. Do you seek the diversion of a gut-wrenching soap opera to play around in? Are you hitting the tables at the casino? Are you invested in high stakes drama?

Monkey too is the great performer dancing in a hall of mirrors. He flashes many mirror faces. His absurdity produces a high comedy. Monkey mixes the real and the unreal, like a Chinese box, like the Mind—boxes within boxes *ad infinitum. When you tire of the chitter-chatter of your internal dialogue ask Monkey to bring you to your essential Mind.*

Try to formulate a method to clear foggy mental attitudes. Do not put your ego at the center of your endless inner dialogue. If you are in a flurry of scrambled thoughts, do not make quick assumptions or conclusions. The product of this kind of brain work is ineffective. Make friends with your Inner Monkey. Keep an eye on her or him. Do you know what your Inner Monkey is trying to tell you right now?

Creativity often means making the unimportant important. Or conversely, taking that which seems greatly important and showing that it isn't important in the least. When a subject is elevated, Monkey kicks the pedestal out from under it and lets the precious creation crash to the floor and shatter. Then it is time to sweep up and toss that idea into the rubbish heap.

Monkey lives in the life of the mind. He is a great artist, musician and scribe. He loves letters, numbers, glyphs, colors and sounds. He takes his thoughts and makes the Book of Dreams. He teaches us how to read the world. He was the first writer and counter. He scribbles his thoughts and spews clouds of paper across the countryside.

Monkey Card counsels you to get involved with some creative endeavor. Now is a good time to cultivate awareness and spike your communication skills—write, paint, sculpt or just have a heart-to-heart with a friend or companion. Use your mind for that which it was intended—creative intelligence.

SNAKE SKIRTED WOMAN
Healer

She is the fearsome rattle doctor. She is the healer, the rememberer of your fate. And she is waiting for you.

The Rattlesnake People begin to shake their tails and make a curious, unsettling whirr. Your heart pounds as the snakesong rattles reach a menacing crescendo. Now you see her. This is no ordinary healer but one who has learned the wisdom and power of the ages. Her skirt is made from snakes in a weave of life merging into death. Thirteen thongs attached to her skirt are encrusted with snails representing the cosmic spiral upon which our galaxy is built. She wears a necklace of hearts and hands reminding us to work to uphold cosmic order. She has the serpent power to strike at your problem with deadly accuracy—only in her case this power is used for healing instead of harming.

You stand before her as she sizes you up, and slowly, down. Then she gives you her diagnosis. She tells you that because of your manner of living and your false beliefs, you have been poisoned. Her job, assisted by the Rattlesnake People, is to cleanse you and free you of this poison. She begins by feeding your energy body with new power to heal physically, mentally and spiritually. Her power glance yields the little lightning, the shaktipat of the goddess. This spiritual energy, not yet recognized by science, is called by many names—*pe, manna, prana, orgone* and a host of others. Snake Skirted Woman carries this quality in abundance and she has the ability to use it.

Snake Skirted Woman also represents blood, the oceanic essence flowing through all humanity. Since she is a midwife, the snake

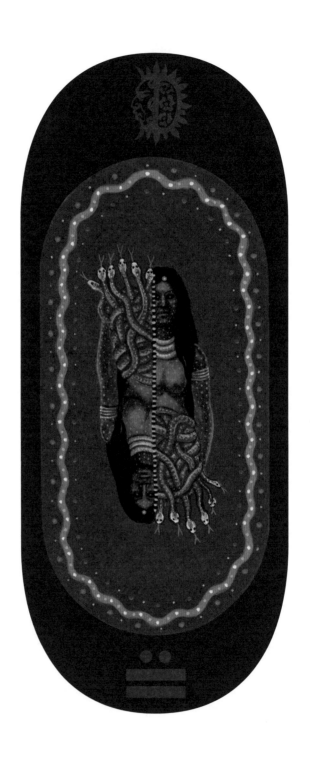

represents the umbilical cord. Her presence brings about quick changes and sudden potent realizations. She demands that you shed many skins in order to reacquaint you with your own deepest levels of healing. Her counsel is to look at the spiritual origin, design and teachings that undergird your problems. She is the great repairer of broken humans.

Snake Skirted Woman may be in the cards in order to heal some family misunderstanding or other problem and to teach an important spiritual truth about your situation. If your question is about health, Snake Skirted Woman may be saying you should consult with alternative healers such as ayruvedic, Chinese or Native American practitioners. Perhaps you need some hands-on work. If you are suffering, she asks you to know that this is the pathway to healing. Suffering is body wisdom. Our pain often restores health.

Snake Skirted Woman is painted white. She gives life but she won't let you forget that life is maintained by death. Disease, in ancient times, was thought of as a sentient being. Today, we call those beings microorganisms. The patient and the healer spoke to the disease as a living friend. Ill health was a supernatural summons. The patient was called to take action to regain his or her health. Snake Skirted Woman counsels that you are the main participant in your healing.

Rattle Doctor Woman can help you alleviate pain on all levels. Let her. She can teach you to strike at your problem with enormous force and solve it. She is on good terms with the master animal spirits. She invokes her powerful animal helpers and puts them to work on your behalf. She demands these creatures use their healing powers to hunt down the causes of any infirmity. Snake Skirted Woman restores you to balance and harmony—healing you. She blows plumes of tobacco smoke across your body. She restores your spiritual connection with your family and to all people. Her job completed, she embraces you and sends you away.

Snake Skirted Woman Card asks you to observe and give yourself over to the rhythms of a truly healthy life. Find a proper diet for

TWELVE

S
N
A
K
E

S
K
I
R
T
E
D

W
O
M
A
N

57

your personal needs. Eat natural and healthy foods and lay off sugar. Get some exercise every day. Make it a pleasure. Take a hike, a swim, or a ride on a biking trail. Snake Skirted Woman may be saying to be careful of some unhealthy relationship or situation. She asks that you search your dreams for their most significant meaning. Lastly, pay attention to your inner as well as your outer needs. Find your heart and hands and use them together to find the spirit of spirits within your health or any other issues. This is the divine wisdom that furthers good fortune at all levels of your existence.

GRASSHOPPER
Mother Dead

The Mother of All, Grasshopper, leads us to understanding.

Before our present creation, all of life was inside the Earth. Grasshopper was the living matriarch of all life underneath. Grasshopper gave life to all beings that lived in this deep and mysterious place, including her human children.

Grasshopper Mother called Parrot. "I will lead all my children up to a New World, a New Sun," Grasshopper Mother said to Parrot. "All conditions are right. It will be a very different world. The way you experience life will be greatly changed. The sky is different. It is a good place I am taking you to, a better place. If you respect one another, everybody can live together in peace and harmony. Go now, Parrot. Tell all the beings of our world to assemble. Get ready to ascend."

And it was so. The great march to Earth's surface was organized. Grasshopper, walking behind and shepherding her children and all sentient life, guided them through tunnels toward the surface of the Earth. "Go on up above," Grasshopper Mother told them. "I will join you when all have emerged."

All the creatures that we know today, the birds, the four-, two- and many-legged beings crawled out to this New World. The New World was stunning in its beauty and richness. There was a new sky with light and it was good. There was day and there was night. There was noontime and there was midnight. There were foods in great variety— vegetation and many kinds of nuts, fruits and berries. The world was abundant with its gifts.

All beings were contented except the humans. The human tribe

TWENTY COUNT CARDS

60

met in secret. "I want to stay in this New World," the leader of the humans said. "Our Mother may force us to return to our old world where we were often cold and hungry. We were always miserable there. I never want to go back down there. Let us destroy our Mother when she emerges. We can chop her up and be rid of her by pushing her back down homeward into the Earth. She will leave us alone and we can enjoy ourselves. What do you say?"

Some humans were reluctant but most went along with this strong leader. In great fear, the humans waited for Grasshopper Mother to emerge. When she entered our present world, the humans fell on her and beat her with sticks and stabbed her with sharp pieces of flint. "Wait!" she cried. "Hear me," she said, managing to hold on to the edge. "I feel my life slipping away. You have destroyed me. Now I am your Mother Dead. For what you have done, all life must now taste death. No one will be able to escape it. With death will come suffering. You will feel sorrow for the loss of those you love. Death and life are now inseparable.

"Earth will become one vast burial ground and the dead will be scattered inside it. You too will one day return to me, your mother, now forever dead."

Grasshopper plummeted downward and the earth swallowed her. She was never seen again. Her small children hop about here on Earth to remind us of our lost creatrix mother.

According to ancient teachings, we must respect all of life or face certain sickness and even death. Insults to the natural world have vast repercussions of which most humans are barely aware. The shaman traditionally communicates with the animal spirits that give humans the knowledge and power to overcome difficulties.

The Mother Dead Card means to be on good terms with the sacred ground. She tells us to enjoy the beauty and satisfaction of being alive. Reverence and protect Earth and all life in it, on it and above it. When we protect the Earth, we protect ourselves and we protect all future life. By learning of Mother Dead's powers and her mysterious teachings, you reclaim the power given by the master animal spirits.

61

Study the ancients for wisdom as this knowledge has stood the test of time. Use sacred technology and deepen Connection. Use prayer. Use ritual. If it works, it is related to everything that works. Touch the sacred ground where our Mother Dead, the mother within our mother, is waiting deep inside our sweet Mother Earth.

T
W
E
N
T
Y

C
O
U
N
T

C
A
R
D
S

FOURTEEN

OCELOT
Sacred Intentions

Smoking Mirror shape-shifts to become the mirror-eyed Ocelot.

Once there was a great jealousy between Smoking Mirror and Feathered Serpent over whose powers of divination were the strongest. Whose vision was going to prevail? The argument became so fierce a war broke out. Feathered Serpent was victorious. He exiled Smoking Mirror to the night sky for six hundred and sixty-six years.

Ocelot is called the Lady of the North, Lady of Darkest Night. She blends with the stars. Scattered across the sky, she is hidden and eludes any pursuer. From this perspective, Ocelot gazed down through the centuries to the oceanic depths. Her sentence served, she plummeted deep into the water. She became one with the Mother of Waters, an aquatic serpent flying through a watery underworld. Twisting, and rolling with the strong currents and tides, she fought her way to the surface. She emerged on the shore and climbed the holy ceiba tree to the very top. To this day she sits among the white flowers and her mirror eyes slice like knives through the darkness.

Ocelot sees and makes perceptions malleable. She stays focused on her sacred intent. Heaven, Earth, and water—the sacred cat can move through these elements with grace and impeccability. The Ocelot path is lonely and one solitary step at a time. When we want to accomplish a goal, we do not have to compromise, but we often have to bend. We have to finesse through the forces blocking our objective. Ocelot teaches us to use our intuition in dodging obstacles. Her great knowledge of the interior of the earth enables her to stalk the surface world carrying the power to shape-shift through many inter-dimensional portals. The

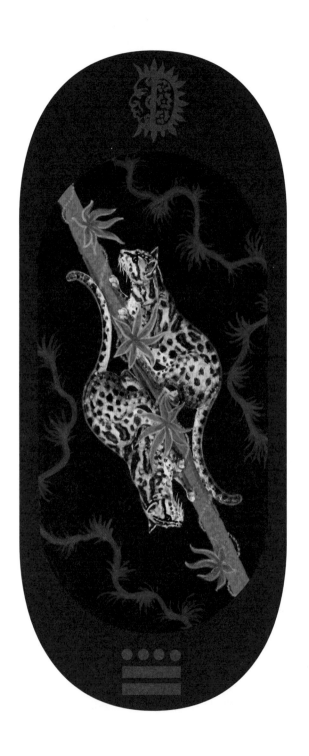

Mayan name for "shaman" and Ocelot are the same.

Ocelot has the power to unite purpose with action. The Ocelot has the lucidity to take action without dispersion of energy. She has a courageous spirit and can walk you through fear. When the path is fraught with danger, Ocelot recognizes the single choice that is necessary for survival. Her total being is accessible—the mind, the body, the emotions. Ocelot brings power from within to triumph over hazards.

Lucidity is not control. It is the ability to confront the reality that is in front of you. It is perfect intention. Controlling is a form of fear, a separating of self from content. Control is the philosophical model and a guiding principle of western thought. However, control is not unified because it is a narrowing of self worth. Losing control, one often feels a loss of self but the loss occurs when using intention in an improper manner. Real intention implies free will, beyond projections, selfishness and wishful thinking. Intent must always be tied with action. You are and you do.

Conversely, Ocelot is not obsessed by action. She takes her time. She knows how to be comfortable waiting. She has discipline and knows how to pace herself. She knows the precise moment to strike. Her beingness and actions are merged into oneness. Without thinking, her intention is realized.

Long ago, before the great Mesoamerican tribes and even before the cave tribes lived the sacred power animals. Monkey, the macaw, the bee, ant and other animals were living in confusion and got into heated arguments. Ocelot intervened and taught the animals Sacred Intent. With intention, each animal's path became clear and they learned to live in balance and harmony.

Ocelot can be gentle or aggressive—a helper or a destroyer. Ocelot loves to play with life and death. She goes straight to the mark. In the hunt, Ocelot makes a just kill. Ocelot is recognized for her inner stillness and effortless effort. Ocelot is centered, confident and at peace. The power gaze of Ocelot is one of force and unshakable will and she sees much that cannot be seen by others.

Some people juggle their eyes. Some hang their eyes in a tree while others roll them along on the ground, hitting them with a stick. Some people throw their eyes to a great distance. Still others give them to the buffalo or even to a tiny mouse. She of the Silver Mirror Eyes is able to penetrate all darkness and divine the future.

Ocelot Card, number fourteen, is a fusion of seven and seven—seven on the left and seven on the right. It signifies magic in the ordinary world and magic through the dimensions. Ocelot is closely tied to Sacred Jaguar and the Sun. The markings on her pelt represent sunspots and other solar activity. Ocelot is the embodiment of cosmic intent. The business of the Sun is to create radiation and light to further the spiritual understanding and awakening of humanity and all other life forms. Conscious intent is supernatural energy stored in the mind.

Ocelot Card appearing in your cards is a fortunate omen. Ocelot, with her spiking mirrored eyes, can give you clarity. Take her eyes and throw them to other worlds and they will come back to tell of unknown futures. Her eyes can track across time. They can trace into the spirit world. Her eyes can climb the sky. Ocelot exemplifies the ability to accomplish the impossible. She is unstoppable and teaches you how to do one thing at a time. Ocelot is asking you if you really want to actualize your intention. Perhaps you are attached to the outcome for if you are, you will never be satisfied. Ocelot knows that each step toward your intention is the intention itself.

Ocelot Card says to quit faking. "What is your true purpose?" Ocelot asks. "What are you doing here? What are you supposed to be doing? By what means can you do it? What price are you willing to pay for the survival of your planet?" Find your true purpose in life. Throw away your old disposable self and get a self living at one with creation. Put your will with the will of the universe. Make a contract with the absolute and do your part. Put your heart and soul into it and go through the motions. Then watch yourself as you cross old boundaries into the covenant and make the impossible possible.

Master Sacred Intentions and you master the world.

EAGLE BOWL
Time

The Temple steps
Are wet with blood
A drugged victim
Lies across stone
And there is sacrifice
The spilling of jeweled water.

A black knife
A human heart.
Taken as an offering
In Eagle Bowl
To Our Sun. Father.

Eagle Bowl is the bubbling cauldron of time.

All calendars, ephemeras, books of time, almanacs, and even Einstein's equations, were hatched in Eagle Bowl. Eagle Bowl Card is number fifteen, and the Mayan symbol for fifteen, three horizontals, speaks of entering upon a third world, a third level of existence. Fifteen is a magic constant and so is time—at least so far. The measure of time is a record of the celestial mechanics of the cosmos. One stage has reached perfection and completion. Another stage begins. Time falls on earth from forever and immediately returns to it. We live inside the flicker of this narrow band.

In the dark beginning, the story is told, the Great One collected all of time and put it in a bowl. The contents of the bowl are incomprehensible.

Time is a stew beyond understanding created by the Master Chef. All we can do is sample it. Eagle, the celestial messenger between earth and heaven, daily announces the rebirth of the Sun. His cry calls the Sun forth. Eagle Bowl is the Turquoise Prince that follows the turquoise trail that leads to the Turquoise Temple. Eagle Bowl takes the complete measure of our breath of life.

Eagle Bowl gives us the power to expand our boundaries and our reality. "Listen, I am what was," says Eagle Bowl. "I am what is and what is to come. Inside of me is everything." Eagle Bowl is filled with wisdom and wondrous beauty.

There is no arrow of time. In life, time is experienced as flowing in one direction, but it is simply our activity in the spatial dimensions that determines time. Time moves in every direction simultaneously. Since time is not linear, it has contours and it is shaped geometrically. Time and space are curved and they look like a bowl. All of time is contained in Eagle Bowl. Time spirals around and around and reconstitutes itself in new phenomena, for Eagle Bowl is the great hollowness that holds this universe.

All of "was not," "is not" and "that can't possibly happen" is said to be lurking in Eagle Bowl. Human beings construct civilizations to foster a reliable and predictable world. Fate often has its own ideas. There is no Paradise that can be constructed inside of Eagle Bowl. There is no Utopia — not now, not ever. We live in our present circumstances.

There is elegance in the poetry and color of time contained within Eagle Bowl. Cultures once perceived our universe as a being analogous to the human organism. The universe has a body, mind and spirit much like our own. Our universe lives, grows old and will die. Intelligence animates the cosmos. Ancient people were obsessed by the cycles we have come to call time. For them, the consciousness of the living universe was real, but finite.

Eagle Bowl Card holds spiritual treasure. Eagle Bowl carries hearts to the sun and shuttles the human soul as it ascends through the thirteen heavens. Eagle Bowl contains many strong and weak suns. Looking into Eagle Bowl, we see the destruction of cosmic eras. We can also see cosmic renewal. And here lies the possibility of your own renewal through the teachings of Eagle Bowl and an understanding of time.

The obsidian butterfly has flown and we all sacrifice to time. But Eagle Bowl can create a cessation of time as well—a gateway to explore your personal truth. Regeneration of spirit informs Eagle Bowl. Walk inside. Reset your setbacks to set-forward. Let Eagle Bowl get you out of time crunches. Eagle Bowl encourages you to dispense with pettiness and to realize your largess of spirit. Fill your tiny portion of Eagle Bowl with good works and a happy life. Inside each of us, the elders tell us, is a gift from Eagle and we are the Eagle Bowl as we send our own hearts into creation.

SIXTEEN

CONDOR
Purification

Condor, the bone cruncher, has a special place in the next world. He is recognized for his service, that of taking on the purification of the world. Great Spirit acknowledges him for purifying the realm of the living by eating the dead. Condor humbly accepted this undertaking when all others of the bird tribe refused.

"Many will fear you," Great Spirit told Condor. "But when they come to my world, the spirit world, they will find you standing next to me."

The Condor in myth and in fact has a unique and symbiotic connection to solar forces. In the dew-damp morning, the birds must wait for the sun to dry their bodies and wings before they can fly. And still, they can't fly until the sun produces the thermal winds that carry them aloft.

It is easy to play with words and ideas, but Condor teaches totality. Condor understands that books and symbols cannot ultimately teach us. They are bricks that wall the mind. Condor has the power to consume our words and our symbols in order that we might know a connectedness of being.

Condor teaches the Sacred Wheel of Death. The east holds the quick passing of the infant, and the south is the mournful death of the child. The west signifies the death of an adult. In the north is the death of an elder, an old person. We all must return to the center of the Wheel of Death—to our own death. Condor knows that all life is on this wheel and yet he never speaks of it. He has no voice box and never makes a sound.

Condor teaches of many kinds of purification—purification of body, mind and spirit. Purification begins with forgiveness. Just as Condor cracks bones, he breaks deadlocks. Condor has the power to make way for clarification. Condor doesn't belong to the world of judgment. To look at a situation in a simple and clean way often means to be misunderstood. You go against what is regarded as the "common sense" of the people.

Condor's number is sixteen. Sixteen separates all things and brings them to purity. The sixteen-pointed star is said to be closest to Creator and so is Condor. Life and death are one to Condor— there is no borderline. Condor circles high and carries a unique vision of our human circumstances. The sky trails of the Condor are isolated because of his special gift. He has a difficult job and he does it. Condor does not kill prey. His survival depends on sighting and consuming the dead. Condor likes thermal currents high in the mountains to spot carcasses. He does not use smell but instead uses acute vision. He engages the putrefaction that the rest of the animal world rejects. Therefore, his immune system is highly effective and bacteria resistant.

Condor has a wingspan of nine feet. His feathers are extremely long and efficient but vulnerable at that length. Bonesetters prized condor feathers as emblems of their occupation. Condor does not wear the robes of ceremony, whether the attire is doctor's whites, the sundancer's skirt or the monk's saffron vestments. For Condor completes the daunting journey to the land of the dead day after day.

Condor engages with little physical aggression within his tribe. Instead, he uses behavior to establish dominance. Condors fly in groups numbering up to sixty. Air speeds top out at fifty-five miles an hour. As the sun heats the mountain air, they fly higher and higher, staying aloft for hours, not beating their wings but skimming along the thermal pockets. The ancients believed the sun sent radiance to the trees, which in turn produced the winds and gave life through breath. Elders teach that Condor is a symbol of reconciliation as he overcomes duality; by eating the rotten, rejected garbage of death, he lives and thrives. The Condor lives for eighty years.

The flight of the Condor casts this divination into a realm where all identity is abandoned. What if you had no religious, cultural, class, ethnic or even gender affiliation? With no voice, Condor has no song. Ask Condor how to bring purity to your question. Life is a great gift. Condor teaches us to live in the present moment with no dead time. Condor energy can set the tone for your future actions.

Condor is chief protector spirit for healers, hospice workers and those whose work leads them to bridge the world of the living and the dead. Emergency personnel, paramedics, police officers and others who confront serious crisis can call on Condor's resilience. It is well to remember that all comes eventually to the altar of purification. It begins in purity. It ends in purity. Let your divinatory question end as it began, in purity.

BALL COURT
Challenges

Go to the Ball Court to honor the forces that put together the universe.

The ball game is played in three worlds—this world and the over-and-under worlds. Events in the Ball Court have a psycho-mystical meaning. With a little imagination we can perceive a triad of worlds simultaneously. The Ball Court was first a spiritual place to pray and honor the ancestor spirits and the vibrant forces that animate the cosmos. We can imagine the spirits of the great warrior athletes as they competed with each other throwing themselves into the fray. In the drama of the Ball Court one could remake the world. The ball was *ollin*, movement, and in its trajectory could be seen as modeling of our own fate and the chance opportunities we are given in life.

Today, Ball Courts lay abandoned across our mound-building empires, a silent testament to our gaming selves. The ball was once in play against the gods themselves. The heroes of our ancestors were great ball players. People loved to tell stories about the players' prowess. Legends abound about the strategies for winning, the skills required. It is no surprise that our society continues to be fixated on the ball court, the players and the game. This passion and competitive spirit continues upon the ball fields of modern times.

Ball Court Card is number *seventeen*, a number signifying move-ment or ollin. Embedded in this number is the entire allegory of the shapeshifting Venus twin and his brother Plumed Serpent in a cosmic epic. The spirits of the great trickster twins inform the ball play with tricky tricks and magic moves in a symbolic struggle for the right to

exist. The magnificence of the play echoes back through time to a life-death struggle with the gods.

Ball Court is an arena. Just as in modern-day football or basketball, there is a place for spectators to sit and watch as the two teams compete with one another. A hard rubber ball is used. The ball, called ollin, is ceremonially fashioned from copal and covered with rubber. The object of this game is to knock the rubber ball through a stone ring. The competition between the two teams is fierce and when the ball is in play the crowd goes mad. It is a game of life and death.

There are three players on each team. The game can be seen as a metaphor for the movement of celestial bodies and the Sun moving in and out of the underworld. At the beginning of the game there was a pageant. Players wearing great rainbow-painted stone yokes paraded in front of the spectators. Rainbow in the sky is the meeting ground of the gods and rainbow's representation on Earth is the Ball Court. Archeologists have found thousands of these stone yokes at burial sites. Obviously, players became the personification of the gods.

Humans have free will. Action in the Ball Court is flowing and mutable. The play shifts in an instant. Everything is in flux. Each moment offers its fullest potential. There are no set laws determining the outcome. In the game people need to keep honed, alert and exhilarated. "And what would life be like without fun and games?" Ball Court asks. "What games are you playing? What are your personal challenges?"

We are all players and we all face challenges. Ball Court teaches us how to make decisive choices and how to be victorious. When you gamble you cannot assume that you will always win. You must accept the responsibility for what happens. You must accept the risk. This means that if you are losing you will discover that all is not lost. Your challenge, the possibility to recover, is still there. Even when the odds are completely against you, remember that the stone ring is a loophole. There is always a way out. Get the ball and get it through the loophole to victory. When you think you have lost, you may still win.

We have chosen to incarnate and be here in these turbulent and momentous times. The rules we were taught no longer work. We must learn to play the game by the real rules. Life becomes less and less predictable and our familiar paths disappear into a vanishing depth. We must learn to face new sets of challenges. When the ball is in play we must sidestep danger and take our best shots.

The spirit canoe floats with the paddlers and the corn gods at the edge of the constelaetion Orion. The group has left the Ball Court to make a journey across celestial waves to see that the great wheels of the cosmos continue to turn. Remember, without opposition there would be no game to play. Our opponents do their best to outplay us and take advantage of every chance to score. When we have the opportunity, we must be brave and do the same. Make our shots count.

Ball Court Card tells you to resurrect your dreams and put them back in play. Don't pay attention to the crowd. Stick to a proven strategy or invent another that is surprising and innovative. Work with your teammates. Always be honorable. Keep your eye on the ball, the ollin, and keep excited about the game. Do not fall into ennui. You can win the game but you must play it for all you are worth. That is your challenge.

Lastly, there is the great and dazzling mirror tree. Upon a branch of that tree is a Ball Court of Mirrors. Here we may play with honor and to the best of our ability but we can never win for here we discover we are only playing against ourselves.

MOTH
Inner Light

A wondrous moth story is told about a shining one who came to Earth to realign the calendar. This was an actual event that took place in the days of human sacrifice. On a day called Flint Daggers, a brilliant light like a small sun appeared in the northern sky. It hovered for many days above the treetops near a native village.

The people gathered in awe and watched this light that rivaled the Sun in brightness. It lit up the night and turned it into day. No one had ever seen such a curious sight. What, they asked, could the nature of this mysterious light be? Is it a star being? Is it a child of the Sun visiting our people?

Dropping down out of the sky, the ball of light descended to the top of a hill and landed in a place where flint was gathered to make arrows, knives and spear points. The light blinded the eyes. The people could only blink in wonder at this amazing incident. A few days later the light separated into two parts. People soon realized a light being had emerged, a god. The being glowed like the Sun. In fear, the people fell to the ground and begged for mercy.

The light being's voice boomed out over the land telling the people they should no longer do human sacrifice. "Because of your disrespect for life, another race is coming who will not permit it. You will be treated cruelly and there will be darkness and destruction. You will know plague and sorrow. Your children will be sold into servitude." And the being of light went on to describe the impact of the ninth hell on the people. "My sons, my daughters, mark well and keep it hidden what I want you to do."

The being of light told of new calibrations for the sacred 260-day calendar and disclosed new and hidden meanings of the Twenty Count numbers and Thirteen Count numbers. The being spoke of their divinatory purpose and of how to use this knowledge in the coming centuries. "I will be watching over you. But I will not come back here until the next world," the being of light said. "So that you may get ready for the New Sun, I will leave moth as a teacher and as an omen of my future return. Learn its wisdom. It is right that I do this."

Flint knife forever afterward symbolized the return of the shining ones. Throughout our oral history, cosmic beings frequently visited Earth. For example, Quetzalcoatl, the sky god, lived with the people and instructed them spiritually, then abruptly left. He returned to the stars on a raft made of snakes. For many years afterward, people went to that very spot and prayed for Quetzalcoatl to return.

There are many tales of godlike beings visiting Earth interdimensionally. One must take a lesson from Moth. Moth guards the doorway for the return of the light beings. She represents reunion. The eyes on her wings represent the ability to see into the supernatural. She is keeper of the many vision-bringing rituals. Moth is keeper of the sacred technology that leads us to other dimensions. Like the moth drawn to fire, our ego burns up. We can then see into another, better world and we can meet with the inhabitants dwelling there.

Eighteen, the number of Moth Card, represents the hidden, and eighteen is also a symbol for inner being. It contains understanding or light. Moth carries this power to envision light, a different plane of being. Reality is much more than merely physical and mechanical observation, although this is certainly a way to describe the human condition. Moth represents the search for light. She is an encircler of light and strives to have union with light. Moth follows the moon in its cycles and she embodies the feminine principle. Reaching your inner light is finding your divine potential. If you seek and find this light you have a spiritual torch to lead you in times of darkness. You have a guide to mark the way.

The old teachers of wisdom said inner light can arrive in subtle ways—a sudden knowing. You may be looking at a beautiful sunset or listening to a symphony. You may be picking up around the house or doing some civic duty. The divine is ignited and comes searing through the dimensions. Your inner light lights your entire being. Your path is clear and the way open.

Moth is twilight twin to butterfly who carries the sunbeams on her wings. Moth begins her journey when the first star appears. She shimmers in the shadows with moon dust on her wings. She asks for your acknowledgement and pity as her tribe is being decimated and going extinct. She knows humans think moths are dreadful. However, Moth is keeper of the Dreamgate. She prepares you through nighttime journeys and instructs you to remember your dreams. Once admitted through the Dreamgate, one is given astonishing divinatory power.

Moth Card is informed with the mysterious, occult powers of women, astral projection and remote viewing, foreknowledge of events and many other numinous abilities. The card speaks of hidden gifts and talents that are not visible and kept secret from necessity. Let Moth make the invisible visible.

There is a language of the night that is different from the language of the day. Moth owns this language. Moth Card instructs you to make friends with all nocturnal creatures and night's good spirits. Come alive at night and dance in the worlds beneath the world. Be completely at home in all universes. Throw open the curtains and allow moonlight to flood into the circumstances or problems you are addressing. The ancients knew magical properties of reflected light from Moon's face. The light of the Moon illuminates aspects of your question not visible in the sunlight. Ancient philosophers and time keepers sculpted imagery into stone that can only be seen in moonlight. Moonlight is the key to unlocking many metaphysical doors—and physical doors as well.

Let inner light be your compass and let Moth be your guide.

COSMIC EGG
Gestation

Gestation is a cyclic period of life replicating itself—of becoming the larger idea within the prime egg and then bursting forth and continuing on to fulfill itself. It is the mystical sphere that contains the complete life process. It is the starting place that seeks and finds fertilization.

First there was nothing.

The egg of eggs was hatched inside of nothing.

Nothing was the cause.

Potentiality gestated until Cosmic Egg cracked open and universes were born.

Bang! A big one—so they tell us.

There are numberless worlds and each one has been gestated and birthed into being. The secret of gestation, as the ancients well knew, is that it never stops. We are in a period of gestation and will be born anew.

The elders point to the dark rain clouds when they want to teach the principles of gestation. "The rain clouds are swelling and pregnant with water seeking release," the elders teach. "Clouds are a form of cocoon or egg," they explain. "When they burst the water comes down."

Cosmic Egg is often related to zero and the number nineteen. Three horizontal lines with the complement of four seed-circles above speaks of a fullness like that of the swollen rain clouds, like that of the pregnant belly at term. The number nineteen dwells in fire. Nineteen

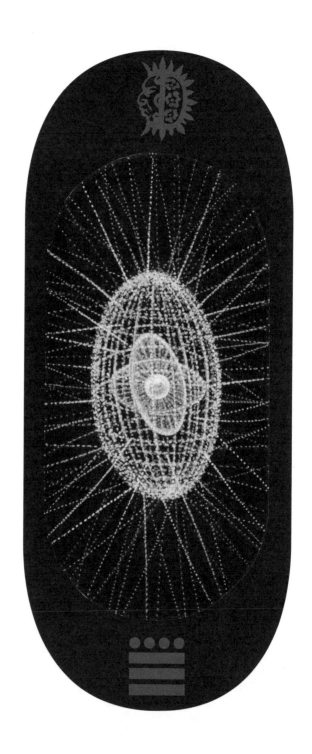

T
W
E
N
T
Y

C
O
U
N
T

C
A
R
D
S

84

facilitates parturition and is associated with the menstrual cycle in women.

Cosmic Egg is the mystery egg of the new creation. Its long cycle is coming to an end. Cosmic Egg holds the vital principle that hatches the light that produces existence. Gestation begins at a point in creation where an agreement is reached that the code of life will initiate. Upon completion, life and spirit burst forth. Gestation organizes the geometrical complexities that lead to the zero point and the birthing of worlds.

Gestation is the evolution of divine thought. Self births self from non-substantiality into substance. Again and again in the maze the pot is set on the three firedogs and the fire is lit. Gestation is the alchemy that takes place inside the divine bowl. Gestation readies the being for the ceremony of life.

The time of gestation is sacred. All movement must be as slow and silent as possible for life is gestating in the Mother's womb. Nothing must be disturbed. Within the Cosmic Egg are our protected and hidden possibilities. Cosmic Egg holds the new and unexpected. Accept and recognize the complete surprise when it comes.

Cosmic Egg also represents the quest for spiritual union. It is a metaphor for fulfilling life's purposes and teaches us to claim a beautiful selfhood. Frequently, we concentrate on the delusions of life and do not see the creations we are unconsciously constructing. Egg teaches that our spirit will one day be liberated and will join with the great Perfection beyond the limitation of time and space. This is the essence of Cosmic Egg.

The oracular field of the Cosmic Egg Card conforms to the resiliency of the elegant design of an egg. Likewise, the divinatory enquiry must cradle Cosmic Egg in a warm and secure nest. Create adaptations, protect, incubate and hatch your inspiration with a determination of the fiercest mother and father. Cosmic Egg reminds us that we, too, can break out of our shell. Prepare a proper environment for your hatchling and fill the atmosphere with a positive attitude.

COSMIC EGG

T
W
E
N
T
Y

C
O
U
N
T

C
A
R
D
S

Cosmic Egg begins the quest for life and beauty. Cosmic Egg is life fulfilling its purpose. Our impediments are an illusion. Spread your Feathered Serpent wings and fly up to touch the highest sky. If Cosmic Egg Card is before you in your reading, pause and think about what is incubating. What is the design of your future? Conceptual models of peace, plenty, cooperation, love and understanding are taught by all the world's religions. The human collective of Earth must strive to realize these teachings. Humanity is incubating and projecting its collective thought forms. Right now, the human projection is gestating for its next wave of actualization. It is imperative we embrace the spiritual teachings of the ages.

WOMAN AND MAN
New Humanity

Here's what happened.

Aba, our Creator, sang a creation song and the song vibrated through the eternity of eternities. The song Creator sang put infinite infinities into our universe and our universe was bound by no boundaries.

A jade ball there was and it floated in the heavens. On the jade ball a tiny green fire burned. Aba saw the gleaming flames and came and blew on them. Clouds of smoke filled the sky and from the clouds ashes fell and covered the jade ball with earth.

Still the jade fire burned. Aba blew on it once more and the smoke rose and created lightning and rain. The rains fell for many days and stopped. There were now lakes, rivers and oceans. Afterward, plants and trees sprouted and began to grow from the earth.

The sun was shining too brightly and the plants began to wither. Aba cut off strands of hair and tied them around the new creation—wrapping the strands around and around and binding it like a ball of twine. This caused shadows to appear for the very first time. The plants grew strong and Aba smiled.

The fire danced happily and smoke billowed upwards. Aba noticed two forms in the smoke and took each of the forms and blew on them and they became New Woman and New Man. Creator rubbed a little earth into New Woman and a little sky into New Man. Creator left the pair to enjoy the divine inspiration of this new world.

When Creator returned, New Woman was restless and completely bored with New Man.

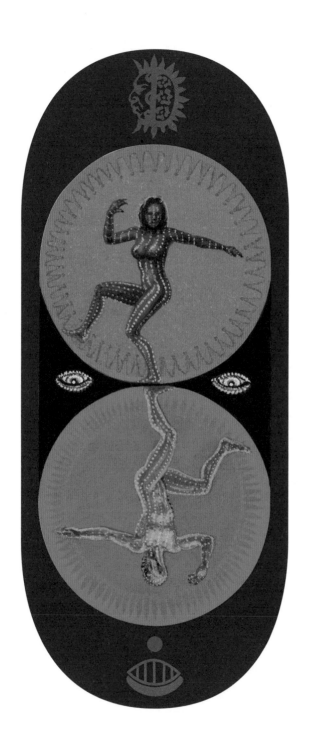

"Ho hum," New Woman said to Creator.

Creator was puzzled. "New Woman, tell me. Why are you unhappy?"

"Lonely," New Woman replied.

"Well, what do you want?" asked Creator.

"I want beauty."

"I will make it so," said Creator.

Aba blew once again on the jade fire. A smoke of different colors danced out in all directions shape-shifting into startling new creatures.

"Animals," Creator explained.

New Woman smiled. "Happy," she said, witnessing all the wondrous new faces of life.

"I must leave you now and go to my land far away beyond," said Aba. "You will imagine I have gone away for good. I have not. Just remember my breath enlivens all of life and everything around you. A part of me is inside of you. The vibrations of my sweet song are engraved upon all of creation. Remember to use my song. Be happy and fulfilled all the days of your life. There is no need to seek me for I am with you always."

Our age is in labor and the birth pangs are coming to term. Our ideas about human consciousness and potential are crumbling. Humanity is finding new tools and new understanding to expand itself. Our old world is dying. As our old world gasps and expires, a new world is being born and a New Humanity is emerging. Beyond what our eyes are taught, beyond the paradigms of culture, there is a truth outside the distortion of the mind.

Woman and Man Card is number twenty, the number of wisdom and realization—the realization only possible to the human family. Twenty carries duality. Twenty is the awakening number and is the sign for divination and ritual. This number asks you to explore both. Twenty also expresses the number of digits allotted to the human.

If you have selected the Woman and Man Card for your reading, prepare to enter a cycle of completion. Finish the old and begin the new. Set your life in order. Make peace with the idea of utter change. As you enter the new paradigm, you may feel anxious or fearful. Go ahead and mourn and process the loss of the old world. Acknowledge with gratitude the old ways that sustained your life.

As 2012 and the emergence of the New Humanity approaches, do your part to create a sustainable future within the context of your situation. Work on those things that won't happen unless you contribute to them and make them happen. If you choose not to participate in creating your future then get ready for the consequences. Better for you to labor for the new world you envision.

We have hidden from ourselves. And so, we come to the paradox of being human. One of us is woman, the other is man and we are equally human. Together we cling to the face of the earth under the forces of gravity. Our muscles and organs are hung on long, bony frames. Arms and legs dangle at our joints. Yet whenever we see a bird ascending effortlessly into the sky, we throw our spirits out of our bodies and fly upward with that bird. Our spirits want to go home to the sun, to the stars.

To heal this great sorrow we meditate on the opposing sides of our nature—the snakebird with one self on the earth and one self in the sky, the light and the dark—the Feathered Serpent. But now, the Feathered Serpent's shadow is covering the earth. It is quiet now, quiet before a new dawn, before New Humanity.

> *Humans are a glimpse*
> *In the dazzling mirror*
> *Carrying the knowledge*
> *Of cosmic oneness.*
>
> *Back to the sun*
> *To the great unity*
> *We go.*
>
> *Our destination, a star.*

THIRTEEN COUNT CARDS

T
H
I
R
T
E
E
N

C
O
U
N
T

C
A
R
D
S

BLACK SUN
Initiation

Black Sun was the first great mirror.

The ancients teach that we are on one side of Black Sun or the other. Awake, we are on one side. Dreaming, another. One represents Mystic Center and the essence of All.

Black Sun has been called Night Eye, Womb Eye or simply Black Eye. It is an eye that closes upon the inner fires of dream. We are admitted across certain barriers where we touch the sacred fires. We become fire beings no longer imprisoned in ordinary consciousness. Each morning, we remember only fleeting shadows of beauty and power. The inability to return from the hidden fire is called death. Death is simply dream without a return ticket.

According to prophecy, Hummingbird will soon fly through the Black Sun and emerge as the great Condor—the smallest of the bird tribes transformed to the largest. This is a double teaching about the transformation of microcosm and macrocosm. Hummingbird is keeper of the rainbow because she flew through the light spectrum and got her shimmering, iridescent colors. All colors together make black. Black Sun is analogous to the pupil of the eye. When we fly into the Black Sun of a realized teacher, there is a transmission of sacred design and we become initiated.

Black Sun existed before creation, before form, and contains all form. Black Sun is the dark, returning matrix, the womb of the universe and represents the power of initiation. The nonphysical resides within the Black Sun, both being and nonbeing. It is what stands behind appearance. Black Sun is the most secret of secrets and it holds the transforming power of initiation.

Behind logic is a mystery that cannot be understood or caught by ordinary means. Initiation is the great leap into the dark abyss of emptiness. Initiation is experienced in the original language that is beyond symbols and words and is communicable only to those who know how to access it.

Black Sun is card number one. Numbers are thought forms that have transcended into real existence. Though multiple, numbers can be decreased to the essence number one. Once one, always one, the ancient mathematicians taught. One is the number of the seeker of truth. Initiation, the first step on your path, requires a pure heart and clarity of purpose. The initiatory journey may be brief or of considerable length. Once one is initiated, the inner world is never the same. Spiritual initiation begins our search to find absolute reality and eternal bliss. A realized person is a mystic warrior who has conquered the enemy of ignorance.

If you have selected Black Sun Card, go inside the quantum emptiness to find a brilliant quantum of promise. If you have been reluctant to start off on a spiritual path, now is the time to do it. You don't have to find a guru or charismatic leader. All you have to do is make your intentions clear. A prayer for initiation sends a cosmic telegram to the Mystery Powers. Because the Power in the Mystery is everywhere, your wish will fly back to you like a black eagle of fire.

The sun of initiation is not an obscure concept but a living truth. It is the doorway into secret worlds. Have no doubt. Black Sun is sending mystical light into your situation. This light can ignite the fires of the mind and spirit. It consumes the ego on the pyres of inner truth. Kick your puny ego down the street like a rusty old tin can because you won't need it anymore. Initiation begins when you become one, when you open your heart to creation and let the Great One work through you.

Black Sun Card awakens lost memory. Light from the Black Sun always gives a simple answer to a complex question. Black

Sun Card challenges you to find the spiritual way. There is a longing of the human soul to find completion and an end to the terrible loneliness of being. Black Sun is the eye in the whirl-pool of wonder drawing you deep into spiritual realms where the puzzle you have created can be understood. Once solved, it asks you to be decisive and self-reliant.

TWO

SMOKING MIRROR
Divination

Enter the mirror that smokes, the mirror of magicians and sorcerers. Smoking Mirror is a seer. He holds a great polished obsidian shield. His asymmetrical face is inhuman, menacing, fearsome to look upon. Here is the keeper of the clouded mirrors of divination. Divination is the reflection of things to come. Reflection is a doubling and is represented by the number two.

"I am the jaguar of the left. I am Smoking Mirror and I have all futures coming to me. I will send your questions into the spirit mirror," says Smoking Mirror, the Lord of Deepest Night. "You have limited yourself and imprisoned yourself within the supernatural darkness of the mirror. Now you seek clarity from the mirror that is smoked. Do you have the strength to accept what I reveal to you?"

Gazing deeply into Smoking Mirror, one transcends the blind acceptance of the status quo. Mirror is a face. Answers have different faces. We might have desire but this desire can be changed within the mirror and become entirely different—deeper and wiser.

Scrying bowls used for divination were found from before the existence of the mound-building empires. These bowls were made of iron ore, hematite, magnetite, iron pyrite and finally, ground and polished obsidian. Mirrors evolved from these divination bowls. Smoking Mirrors were gorgeous, convex and were at the epicenter of this long oracular tradition.

Smoking Mirror shows us a world that can be looked into, but not passed through. Mirrors were spirit gates, passageways for supernatural beings to enter and return. Mirrors were said to be eyes, faces, shields, the Moon and flowers. Mirror-Reptile-Eye has the power to curl along surfaces and penetrate shining and reflective faces. Priests and priestesses wore mirrors on their chests and on their backs. Mirrors were considered to be the most sacred of objects. Priest and priestess astronomers looked into black obsidian mirrors. These mirrors were telescopes used to note sun spots and record the regularity of this activity. Solar flares were measured and correlated to events on earth.

The shadowy mirror holds it—the darkness hidden in darkness and our own light hidden in light. How easy it is to distort our position in the cosmos. We are always projecting ourselves from the hidden depths of who we believe ourselves to be. Inside the latent depths of Smoking Mirror is a distortion. That distortion is you. The power of Smoking Mirror is to give you back your true self by understanding your distortions. Smoking Mirror shows you that the negativity laid upon us from without can be overcome from within. This is Smoking Mirror's great teaching.

The value of Smoking Mirror has been lost to modern civilization because we do not recognize his usefulness. As children we are taught to collect a series of responses that bring desirable results. We rely on this. We don't experiment with these reactions. Smoking Mirror says, "I will help you cross over to find the new approach. Come dance with me within the black mirror of understanding."

The image of the illusion is lost in the smoky mist—in the labyrinthine hypnotic darkness. One sees beyond the surface deep in the darkness where directions are non-existent. Nonetheless, one discovers direction within the paradox and the mystery. It is the mirror where one is lost in order to be found. It is the red mirror, the mirror of sudden fiery brightness. Against any apparent logic, you may discover a different, more profound logic.

Smoking Mirror Card is the oracle within the oracle. Smoking Mirror tears up any map or rulebook which makes us sure of what we do. We have just one life, and the more we live with our life and our death, the more we can understand the richness of life. Smoking Mirror tells us that we are always mirroring. Smok-

ing Mirror asks if you are afraid to look, to admit your ignorance. Have you been pretending to have answers you don't have? If so, your task becomes mirroring back truth.

If the lord of deepest night card has limped into your reading flashing a smoking mirror on his forehead, look deep into your question for its mystical meaning. The obsidian mirror captures signatures of unseen futures on its face. All mirrors are the Sun's relations and seek to reflect justice—true justice. Inside the conjuring smoke of the mirror is your true reflection. Hidden in the smoke is a luminous being—you. Gazing in the deepest darkness, a shining path appears—a path with an unexpected answer.

T
H
I
R
T
E
E
N

C
O
U
N
T

C
A
R
D
S

CORN MOTHER
Blessings and Nourishment

To the peal of copper bells
Corn Mother and Moon Goddess
Walk hand in hand
Scattering sacred corn pollen
Calling the rain.

"I am the one who sprouts from the rich loam—with sprouts streaming out from my knees. I must live to give food," says Corn Mother. Corn Mother is abundant and generous. Dressed in her husk vestments she embodies the harmony of self and universe. Corn Mother sends thoughts of love and nourishment to the human community. Any kind of activity can bring amity if it is related to blessings and the roots of life. Celebrating Corn Mother calls beneficial spirits into your life as you dance and flow with life's sustenance. She is the discovery of gifts from the earth and related to many plants. Her brothers and sisters are avocado, chili, flowering tobacco, cotton of many colors, morning glory, water lily, amaranth, cacao and others. She is the discovery of universal beliefs concerning nourishment of self and others. The number three rules the vegetative world and farming.

She is the First mother. The gods made the first humans from ground corn. As such, we were born to oneness. Humans were smarter than the gods so the gods clouded their vision. Humans could no longer see the complete truth but Corn Mother can make our way clear.

● ● ●

T
H
I
R
T
E
E
N

C
O
U
N
T

C
A
R
D
S

We send thanks to Our Mother of the Precious Stalks. She instructs you to thrive. She holds the hand of Grandmother Growth. She gives us the milk from her breasts. She is our holy mother and protector. There are many devotional ceremonies honoring Corn Mother. Corn is of many colors. Her face is red, yellow, black and white. She is Mother of us all, say the old ones.

The amicable spirit of Corn Mother is dancing over the sown fields. Life is prosperous and good. Pushing up from the dirt, green corn to ripe corn, she sways gracefully to the rhythms of nature. She is evoked for her blessings—ear to the Moon. Corn Mother attends us with her bountiful harvest, from birth and through the course of our lives. The ancient people kept sacred corn bundles containing a perfect ear of corn on their family altars and opened them when they wanted to celebrate their blessings and stay in the good graces of nature. They fed the ear with smoke and felt a close connection with Corn Mother. Her fruitful spirits are our wellwishers. *Corn Mother speaks of increase and prosperity.*

Corn is a lesson in multiplication. Originally, Corn had but one kernel. But the ancient agrarians discovered some with two kernels. They planted these as seed corn. When the plant matured, some had three kernels. These were again planted. Each time the planters took the ears with the most kernels until they produced a full ear of corn. Corn Mother multiplied the harvest for her children. She teaches that humanity, working collectively, can manifest any reality.

Corn Mother is the perfect expression of love and wisdom. She bestows her blessings to others with love. She asks you to do the same. Give freely of your good will and blessings. To bless is to recognize the living divine spirit. Bless others. Bless their life, work, and path. When we bless freely it returns to us. Bless your problem, quest or question. Love is a great blessing and you are blessing others all the time when you love them. Allow Corn Mother to be expressed through you. Love and support others. Corn Mother is the inexhaustible harvest coming into form. And she is your holy mother and protector.

No matter what is going on in your life, Corn Mother comes to your rescue. If times are difficult for you, remember her nourishing truth—the gift of her many-colored treasure. In times of need, call upon Corn Mother's help. Oh, swaying mother, give us your strength and sweetness. Let her help you preserve your health, peace, love and harmony. In days of disharmony and even if people judge you harshly, seek Corn Mother's support. Even the sting of criticism can be a blessing if you learn from it.

Corn Mother can help you improve any situation and find the richness in it. She always seeks to give you abundance, nourishment, and to improve your general circumstances. If you have drawn Corn Mother, count and recount your blessings. She often foretells immediate good fortune. If your question is about business, chances are you will receive some gain soon. Rest easy. Be like the yellow butterfly skipping over the green corn. Be optimistic. Be cooperative. What you seek is materializing.

TEMPLE
Sanctum

We search for the Sanctum within the four-sided Temple of Self. Four is the magic number of completion. The Sanctum represents the complete understanding of our spiritual purpose and a realization of our highest self. This is our search and our destiny.

The heart of the world was a huge emerald with a serpent and an eagle engraved upon it. This stone was a symbol for the Temple. The serpent and bird symbolized the Feathered Serpent. The Feathered Serpent, Quetzalcoatl, built four temples, each facing a different cardinal direction. The eastern temple was built entirely of turquoise. The southern temple was built of pink seashells. The western temple was built of white seashells. The northern temple was built of precious blue-green quetzal feathers. These four temples represented the quarters of the world. Each segment harmonized and aligned the seeker with cosmic forces.

Each temple taught an aspect of the bearing of Venus to the Sun. Temple taught how these celestial phenomena correlated to life on earth. From these correlations came a system of divination and structure that formed harmonious cultures. Our age is the embodiment of all four previous Suns, and as such, we have invented time. But time as we know it will end with the coming of the next Sun.

Temple represents the impulse to seek a spiritual path. Jaguar guardians stand at the door hidden within invisible planes. Quail dart and whirl in the courtyard. A floppy-eared rabbit races by. A pursuing coyote soon follows. Quetzal birds preen themselves on the limb of a lush tree. A tapir in procession with a peccary saunter toward a

• • • •

flowering bush. Four eagles soar on wind currents and give shrill cries. A sleek puma traipses through the dense foliage and disappears out of sight. A dove coos and an owl hoots a throaty *woo*. An elegant blue heron pecks open a shellfish and in a lily-covered sacred pond, a silver fish jumps in the air and makes a splash.

The temple breathes. It is a living entity. It teaches of the coming ages. Inside the Feathered Serpent's temple are masses of flowers, feathered hangings and mosaics of precious stones. Whatever temple Quetzalcoatl visits, the air is filled with sweet perfume that delights the senses. All manner of singing birds keep him company.

Temple points to our place of origin. Temple is a world within worlds. A Temple networks with every other Temple. A temple in Guatemala connects with an Earth temple in Ohio. All temples are related energetically. There are temples of every size and description. There are sacred earth mounds which were temples. Some Temples are ancient and falling to ruin, with twisting vines growing over their broken faces. Others glint in the sun and are built of solid marble. Of the known Temples, Temple of the Sun and Temple of the Moon are the most famous. Then there is the Temple of the Jaguars and Temple of the Magicians, the Temple of Warriors and Venus Observatories, and so on. There are many thousands of temples. These monuments all have one thing in common. Contained within their sacred geometry is a secret place that takes one into the deepest reaches of the human spirit. This hidden place is called the Sanctum.

Temple graces the ages. The Temple path to the Sanctum is so simple and clear that it can't be seen. Normal mind perceives many intricate paths and therefore no path. We say that there is no Sanctum. The Sanctum has vanished or never existed at all. There is no Temple. Temple is a dead monument of a forgotten time and Sanctum is an absurd myth.

Yet many people are playing the Temple game, seeking the most sacred Temple of all and trying to find its Sanctum. Teachers often instruct one that the search for the mystical Temple with its hidden Sanctum is like being at the threshold of a great maze. The maze reminds us that courage is our best friend and fear is our worst enemy.

●●●●

Inside the maze we encounter every sort of trap. We twist and turn and go down blind corridors only to hit a stone wall. No matter the obstacles, we must continue. One day we discover that the Temple is as close as our breath. Truly, the Temple and its hidden mysteries were and always will be. You have visited the Temple Sanctum many times. You simply did not recognize it.

All games have rules. The first rule of the Temple game is that you must win or lose before you can quit playing. You must find the Sanctum or die trying. There can be no cheating in the Temple game. You can't claim the powers of the Sanctum unless you have them. Some players give up and try to return to where they started, but this is impossible. Some players find the Sanctum without any effort while others struggle to no avail.

You may think you have withdrawn from the game only to realize it was a time-out. Play or be caught forever in the maze. Judge yourself in relation to other players and you are utterly lost. The more convinced you are of winning, the more ensnared you become within the twisting corridors and the false avenues of the maze.

If you have drawn Temple Card, you have been given a map to the Sanctum. The map directs you to the topmost part of the Temple, a place with seven doors. There you discover the true entrance. You squeeze inside to find utter darkness. Crawling, you make your way along a narrow, uncomfortable tunnel. It curves subtly this way and that way and it becomes very disorientating. In the midst of your confusion you see a green glow—a light at the end of the tunnel. Getting there, you realize you have entered the Sanctum.

Dwelling within the Sanctum of Sanctums is a jewel glowing with green light—the heart representing a sacrifice of flowers. It is the green sun, the modeler of our creation. One cannot gaze upon this jewel without obtaining wisdom. The walls are lined with goddesses and gods bathed in the green light. These sacred old ones appear to be alive. There are many colorful paper headdresses striped with rubber and removed only for sacred ceremony in deep woods, at the top of mountains, in secret caves and near sacred cenotes. There are holy books and ephemera.

Each year, the Serpent-That-Falls-Downward, the ancestral rattle-snake, descends along the edges of the Temple steps reminding us of the Great-Power-From-Above originating from the Shaking-Tail-Of-Stars.

T
H
I
R
T
E
E
N

C
O
U
N
T

C
A
R
D
S

The energy and power of the Temple is not a myth but a living reality. The diving god is coming to your aid now. The spiritual master is bringing you secret knowledge that has been lost to the ages, which can be put to work immediately. The flying serpent brings the power to give you wisdom and protect you from evil. It brings extra-perceptional powers to see what is needed in your situation. In the days to come, reach for the highest and give each project your best shot.

Temple Card suggests that you may have to search for the divinatory meaning in concurrent events that are relevant to you. Stated another way, an event happening far away is just as important to you as what is right in front of you.

Temple Card signifies a divine space. What you seek is near at hand.

There is a power, a non-personal presence.

This presence is not a thing to be named.

Temples are built on a cosmic model. This unnamable presence is the reason temples are built. It is for this—the unspeakable—we seek.

The Sanctum is the home of this sacred un-thing.

HAND WHEEL
Offering

Many teachings are held in the Great Hand, the hand of the God of Gods. Duality is complementary and not opposed when in the hands of the Great Being. The Great Hand is not absolute but interdependent holding all so-called opposites. The First Hand grasps the conch shell, the instrument yielding the first divine sound, the wind jewel. The Second Hand holds the sacred grass sphere—life lived in balance within ordinary reality. The Third Hand is the Truth Hand sheltering the tobacco leaf. The Fourth Hand holds the obsidian knife, the human-held power to give or take life. Five is the number of the hand.

Consider the wonders that have been built by human hands—the great works of beauty and architecture, the pyramids and temples of the ancient world, and the great monuments in front of us today. Hand Wheel speaks of human balance and striving for fulfillment. Hand, particularly the thumb, is related to Venus. A single hand symbolizes male right-handed and female left-handed groups of five. Stated simply, the left hand is related to the sacred and the right hand is related to everyday jobs, the mundane. The left hand is the spiritual hand. The right hand is the dirt-under-the-fingernails profane hand.

The members of many secret groups and societies correspond to the various digits of the hand. Fingers, including the thumb, are called planets. Each has specific powers. The Venus digit, the thumb, symbolizes the teacher, knowledge carrier or holder. Thumb is ruler of the groups and the central person of authority. Thumb's character is

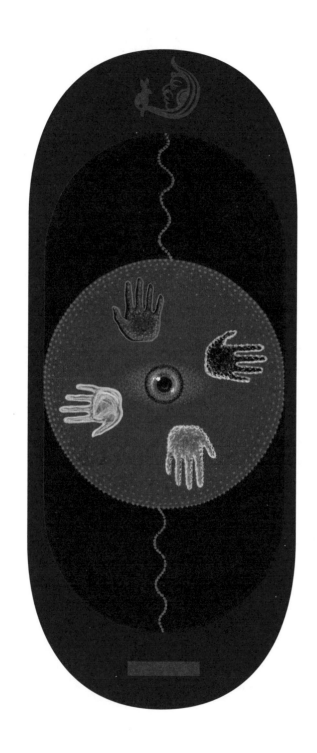

T
H
I
R
T
E
E
N

C
O
U
N
T

C
A
R
D
S

from the ether, void or empty space. Thumb is the power of Feathered Serpent, the material manifestation of the universe. All must come to this digit in order for magical combinations to occur.

Hand Wheel Card tells you to live life with a positive attitude and put your hand to life's challenges. A pipestone hand seeks union. A flint hand seeks truth like an arrow. A crystal hand bestows light. An obsidian hand is introspective and acts from deep inner knowing. The left hand has a heart and correct use of the hands brings good fortune. They are the harmony of hands, the trust of hands, the balance of hands, unselfish, detached hands—hands with flexible fingers and limber thumbs. Remember fingers and thumb oppose each other and this is what makes the hand function.

The secret of the hand is the secret of fulfillment. Hands represent our gifts and our service. Hands give and hands take. Hands teach us how to avoid mistakes. Gentle hands are the loving hands, hands that are willing to let things be and not stamp their will on the situation. By these hands we are touched with blessing and nourishment. To reach out and link your fingers with another is an act of love and acknowledgement of sisterhood or brotherhood. Gentle hands know that life is transitory and we are here conditionally. When your hands are open and giving, it denotes a steadfastness of heart and a permanence of commitment. The hand and the heart working together lead you to happiness.

Hand Wheel Card asks you to look at your own hand. Where is it pointing? What is it grasping? What are you willing to release? Are your hands working toward a goal? Or even, what is it your hands are doing during the course of a day? Clap your hands together and give encouragement and applause where it is deserved. Encouragement is a tonic to those who are stumbling on their path.

Hand Wheel Card tells you to reach for the things you need with no hesitation. Bless yourself. Always be generous, hospitable and comforting. Hand Wheel asks you to observe and see what is needed and then to meet those needs. How long has it been since you have embraced a child or loved one? Have you been withholding affection? Do you need to hold the hand of a person going through hard times or someone who has faced a loss? Hand Wheel Card asks you to share your gifts. You are being asked to give a hand where it is needed. You are being asked to touch the lives of others in a hands-on way. Put your hands to work immediately for reasons you should already know.

SPIRIT CANOE
Journey

Canoe represents a spiritual journey, and the number six represents the six spatial dimensions. Journeying is our only option, because life itself is a journey. We have our spirit companions.

Old Jaguar Paddler sits in the fore of the Canoe and is expert at nighttime travel. Old Stingray Paddler sits in the aft and is skillful at daylight navigation. The paddlers are rough old men, rarely seen without a cigar in their mouths. They represent day and night opposition but they work in tandem. Their paddling strokes are deep, easy and smooth.

The Old Paddlers shuttle the spirits and medicine animals back and forth between the spirit world and the human realm. They are the reliable boatmen who bring the spirits you request into your vision. They navigate all dimensions with ease and skill. Old hands at all conditions—they face storms and tempests with confidence.

Times have changed. Now a journey across the world begins with checking on your frequent flyer miles. Still, it is a magic journey. Canoe glides down-river through waters of awe and mystery. Canoe can mean going across the street for lunch or a lifetime of spiritual seeking. On your journey, you sit with the Alligator or Horned Snake. You converse with Scorpion. You reverence the Morning Star and Evening Star. You honor the Great Mother in all her guises.

Spiritual wayfarers have always existed. Get your paddle in the water and start stroking. Canoe can be a vehicle to visionary worlds. Do not think of your spiritual journey in grand terms. It can be very simple. Your spiritual journey might be sweeping a floor or donating

your time to hospice, working for your family or supervising children at a playground. The face of Creator appears when you are doing ordinary things.

Spirit Canoe symbolizes the journey between worlds. A journey implies movement—either without or within. Each person we meet along the way is also on a journey. We are all making the voyage. You are a wayfarer upon a journey of no return. You may be in a fast or slow canoe. You may take a direct route or choose a slower one. Though we cannot return to where we began our journey, we always end where we started. This journey is amazing and mysterious and it is called life.

In an ancient ceremony, an initiate was seated in an actual canoe with two Ocelots, or shamans, who represented Old Jaguar Paddler and Old Sting Ray Paddler. The initiate was put in an altered state and, sitting between the two guides, journeyed into the spirit world. Here, he retrieved information from the spirits about his journey.

In the good company of Old Jaguar Paddler and Old Sting Ray Paddler, the initiate returned to the everyday world. But now he was different. He was energized spiritually. He was resolved to help the people. Within his fundamental nature was a new power to face life with hard work and courage.

Spirit Canoe Card advises you to remember that your journey is unique and important. Your life will take you through turbulence and whirlpools, through storm and calm. We are all seekers on a voyage of discovery. Do not let your boat drift into the waters of angst and indifference. Point your prow in the direction of spiritual wisdom. Have a venturesome attitude and firm resolve. Go relentlessly into the farthest reaches of your heart and soul.

In ancient times, when sailing on the dark seas there was always a person known as a "grounder." A grounder was analogous to a navigator. On the darkest night with no light or star to be guided by, a grounder could hear the ocean songs and locate the boat's position in relation to land. A grounder knew all the music of the oceans. A grounder could always lead you safely to your destination.

T
H
I
R
T
E
E
N

C
O
U
N
T

C
A
R
D
S

Do not drop your paddle. Stay balanced. Do not let your craft be capsized in torrential waters. Keep stroking. Who will be waiting for you in the Land of the Blue Hummingbird? When you are in a fogbank of trouble, who will navigate you home? Be sure to have a grounder onboard.

Spirit Canoe Card signifies your personal journey and points to the help you are getting from cosmic forces. The Spirit Canoe floats with the paddlers in the night sky. These beings are always reminding us that the journey is forever and that life is a spiritual adventure. On your journey you always have the opportunity to reverse and realign. Then, go forth once more with daring and power.

That is the message of Spirit Canoe.

WOMB CAVE
Fertility

The chanting of souls
seeking incarnation
rippling the star-clouded path
shimmering, shivering
seeking the fertile chamber.

Inhale
precious treasure
the first breath.

Exhale
measure
birth.

Seven, the most magical of numbers, whispers secrets concerning the Cave of Seven Seeds. The Womb Cave was inside a legendary Mountain of the Quetzal and contained seven chambers. This cave was dedicated to She-Of-The-Jade-Skirt. Because of the watery nature of the human womb, her spirit was present at all births and baptisms. The cave was used as a ceremonial space because fertile and germinating powers were concentrated within its walls. Inside this cave, initiates underwent a spiritual birthing. The umbilicus was cut and they were severed from their former lives.

Beneath the Pyramid of the Sun there is a Womb Cave. A biochemical link exists between the Sun's radiation and the production

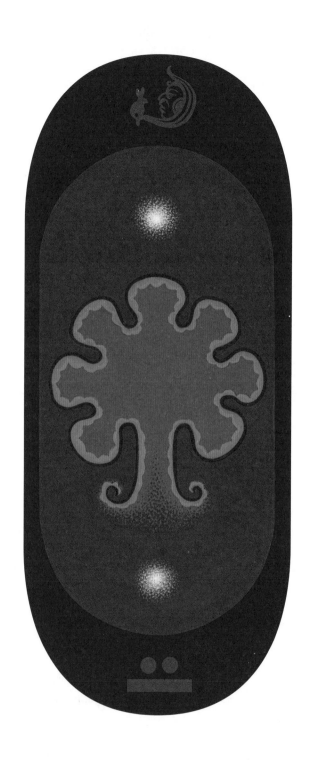

of female fertility hormones. A woman's cycle is twenty-eight days, which corresponds exactly with the Sun's twenty-eight day cycle of rotation. Hormones vary in women due to solar energy. Geomagnetic forces interact with sunlight to stimulate the hypothalamus and the pituitary gland causing menstruation and ovulation.

Humanity was born of the Womb Cave. The Womb Cave is the reflection of within just as life becomes a reflection without. Here the fetus begins its journey into the realm of possibility. The ancient people grasped these truths thousands of years ago. Their tireless observation of the universe paid off. Looking skyward they found answers. They unlocked the mysteries of fertility. Womb Cave holds the void—the eternal stillness of night, and has been likened to a cup—not the cup itself, but the principle of emptiness within it. Womb cave is the intersection of the collaborative forces of life, birth and death. Womb Cave is the inner chamber containing the sacred involuted female, the threshold to all worlds. Her inter-dimensional architecture of fertility and birthing is the Temple of the Mother Goddess. Womb Cave's mystery is revealed in the courage of birth. She is the runway and furnishes the coordinates for takeoff.

The old ones revered fertility. Special ceremonies were held for young women when they reached their first menstruation and became fertile. These women were honored because of their sacred capacity to extend the lineage of their people into the future. Without fertility life stops.

Many ceremonies celebrate Gaia. Inherent in many rites, one is reborn and renewed, as in an emergence from the womb. Maternal love nurtures us, sustains our planet and supports life. In death, we are lowered back into the womb of earth.

We pray for the continual fertility of Great Spirit Mother for she is the matrix of creation, the keeper of rebirth. She existed before our personal attributes or mental scripting. We seek the Womb Cave for it holds the fluidity of the unborn and uncreated self, a place of reconnection to the principles of elemental being. Within the Womb Cave, the holy heat meets with the void. In the search for light, the dark matrix becomes the light itself. This is the origin of our being.

The Womb Cave Card points to your place of origin and offers you a shelter from which to explore new things, to have new experiences, to risk. Fertility is an emphatic "YES!" to life. Let Womb Cave reawaken your slumbering dream. This card speaks of the winding, intricate caverns of the heart. Fertility is reaching out to limitless possibility and into an ever-widening circle. Womb Cave holds the secret to continual nourishment and recreation. With Womb Cave Card one must set the conditions for germination and the creation of form for an important idea or desire. This means that your deepest needs must be met and put away in the fertile depths of productive emptiness. Fertility is divine trust and Womb Cave Card calls out for spiritual unity.

ADVISORS
Advice

There are inherent truths hidden in the fabric of reality. Ancient experts were given the task of unraveling these truths and giving advice. There were advisors who were priestesses, priests, sibyls, seers, prophets, astronomers, dreamers, dancers, scholars and many other kinds of specialists. The ancient advisors knew how to gaze into flames, bones, smoke, leaves, crystals, clouds and animal behavior, and how to mirror their unheard voices.

Eight is the Advisor Card's number. The number eight has achieved knowledge and authority. As such, eight becomes a guiding number. In the ideal, Advisors guide and assist one in the process of evolving to a higher state. The ancient calendars were divided into eight parts and charted eight Venus counterclockwise positions in alignment with Earth. The number eight can be very lucky.

Advisors can help you shape a strategy for radically altering your field of play. If you seek advice, listen to plants, animals, trees, elders, minerals, ancestors, spiritual teachers or other sensible experts. Advice is germane to the surroundings.

Learn to heighten your awareness of the immediate. See with new eyes the scene unfolding around you. The signs are waiting for your interpretation. Pray, meditate. Teach yourself a divinatory system. Take responsibility for your actions. Teach children that they are capable of conscious decision-making and do not have to be the victims of cultural bias and conditioning.

The world is alive when you respond to the synchronicity of each moment. Animals, the weather, trees and plant spirits offer you the

T
H
I
R
T
E
E
N

C
O
U
N
T

C
A
R
D
S

wisdom of the ages. There are countless stories of human lives saved because someone "paid attention."

Advisors are related to four different levels of understanding—emotional, physical, psychical and spiritual. Good advisors minimize stress. Advisors tell us that life is process and we need to get past our difficulties. We need to release and not cling to problems.

If you are simply looking for practical advice, there is a rich landscape of advisors in offices and libraries. Do some intelligent digging to find the right advisor. Good advisors are solvers and not a hidden furtherance to your problems. In other words, they don't string you out.

The Advisors Card may suggest that you have inadequate information about a given situation. It may indicate the need for concentrated analysis and planning. It says to be relentless and thorough in your pursuit of the facts. Ask yourself, "How do I get organized to pursue my intentions?" Is there an objective observer or wise person you can draw upon for support?

An advisor can act as an advocate for a particular point of view. A true advisor teaches one how to become aware and how to avoid inner conflict. The true advisor's great gift is the recognition of every aspect of a problem. Advisors teach us how to face into both light and darkness and that means to discover your real power within.

Divination is such a tool. For instance, what advice does the puma have for you? Does the puma point you to a new role within the question? Eagle sees the complexity of any situation and sees the need for adjustments. Snake is wise and grounded and can find the exact spot within a question to focus energy. Wolf may suggest you seek advice from a recognized authority.

On the other hand, you are the authority you seek.

Advisors Card tells you to listen to the advice that is all around and to access your deepest knowing. Do not expect Advisors to provide you with a complete answer. This card instructs you to examine your advice carefully and look critically at what is working for you and what is working against you. Obtain clarity and then act upon your understanding. The Advisor you seek is within.

T
H
I
R
T
E
E
N

C
O
U
N
T

C
A
R
D
S

WORLD TREE
Centeredness

When you sit beneath the limbs of the sacred tree, light dapples the earth and you are feathered by Sun Eagle and Hummingbird with gold, green, yellow and crimson. The Galactic Tree is the giver of a new light of consciousness. The mystical Tree of Life is complete. Venus has risen over the branches of this glorious Tree.

World Tree is calling her children to come and find refuge and renewal. Come and rest under my branches. Here you will find communion. All are welcome at the base of the healing tree, the medicine tree of the people. "I am sacred," she says. "Use me for your spiritual purposes."

Long ago, Turkey and Tree had a contest to see who could give the greatest gifts. Tree won with her first breath.

Honor the Sacred Tree, the breathing tree, for she literally gives you life. Tree embodies completion and perfection, which are qualities of the number nine. Where there is a tree, there is holiness and power. Each and every Tree has ritual and ceremonial importance. A tree binds the four directions of the cosmos together. The roots bind together the four sides of earth. Trees have a language and they speak to one another and this mystical line of communication exists between humans and trees. Humans give their sacred gifts to trees because they are a direct connection to the Galactic Tree.

Go to the tree. Put your hands against the trunk and pray. Thank the tree for your life. Trees have cosmic healing powers. Sit under trees. This act restores psychological calm and mental clarity.

The branching and flowering tree is the holy tree at the center of the Seven Spheres or Worlds. There are more roots than branches, say the old ones when they are teaching the law of correspondence. Trees must be rooted as well as reaching. What is above is also below. World Tree says, "Come to the perfect center to the great indwelling power."

She is the spirit of all trees. The roots of the World Tree go to the absolute bottom of the universe and the branches reach to the absolute top. This tree contains the principle of all trees and yet it does not contain the principle of all trees. It is the sprouting tree of the beginning and yet it has no beginning. It is beyond time but it is also in it. It is the fallen tree of the ending and yet it never ends. It is forever beginning and ending and between the uppermost branches and the deepest roots exist countless worlds and each world contains infinities of others.

World Tree is the Sacred Tree and stands at the living center of the Nation and the world. She is the tree of council. The trunk is the connection of the Earth below and sky above. She is eternally embraced by a double-pyramid of light. The two flower eagles, hummingbirds, bring a sunbeam and attach it to the rainbow. The light is ethereal and purifying. The rays that bathe the tree are creative as well as re-creative, because of its double nature—male and female.

The four elements are in the tree. There is water in the Earth, and radiation from the sun moves through the air. The holy tree is a place for celebration and dance, a place of sacrifice. It is a refuge of harmony and universal order. Is it any wonder that so many sages have received enlightenment at the base of a Sacred Tree?

The World Tree represents fullness of mind and spiritual reaching toward the ultimate. Adepts have always sought the exquisite blossoms on the Tree of Life. Hovering near the flowering tree, hummingbirds are a sign of fruitfulness and well-being. Tree energy protects children and assists them in their daily life's journey.

World Tree Card indicates steady future growth because of your well-rooted actions. It presages the bearing of fruit from your labors, the good fruit from the good tree. And to taste of this fruit is to taste and realize new possibilities. Go ahead and sample the sweet fruits from this magnificent tree. The World Tree always speaks of balance within the situation or question and suggests ways you can create it. Let this sacred tree teach you how to be yourself—to grow and nourish in stately grace. The dew-jeweled leaves are sparkling in the morning of life. With this spirit tree you can be perfect and complete. Let wholeness and sacredness emanate from you. Become one with this great Tree of Life.

TEN

WOOLLY MAMMOTH
Ancestors

Our ancestors are sacred. The number ten symbolizes our ancestors who have crossed over to the next world. They have completed the journey of one through nine. Ten represents their transition to the next world.

Woolly Mammoth asks you to awaken your genetic memory—the code of life you have chosen to manifest. Life gave you life. And before your mother and father, there were other mothers and other fathers stretching back into the dim past. Woolly Mammoth asks you to be conscious of the next seven generations for we will one day have the distinction of being ancestors. It is certainly our hope that future generations will honor us and remember us.

Native America and Native Mesoamerica know full well that human history can be destroyed by disease and genocide, and gaping holes can be left in the fabric of people's lives. The transmission of information from the older generation to the next can end suddenly. The doors between two human eras are slammed shut with a horrifying finality. However, children are born. And, with the first breath they take, they sense the presence of their ancestors.

Woolly Mammoth teaches that ancestors are always near.

Our ancestors are our legacy. It is dangerous to ignore your heritage—your birthright. It doesn't matter what that birthright may be, if your ancestors were good or evil, ignorant or realized people. They survived and are a link to you. Your ancestors call for acknowledgement and ceremony. Heed that call.

ONE

T
H
I
R
T
E
E
N

C
O
U
N
T

C
A
R
D
S

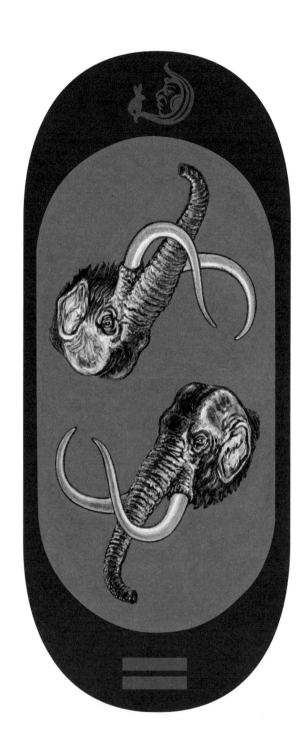

By singing sacred chants, we can reach real people in forgotten time. There is a continuum of time beyond life and death. You carry it. Find the lost strands of your ancestors' legacy in order to weave a new tapestry. Honor your ancestors because they are your roots. They give us different levels of knowledge passed down through the ages.

Time can transform the shape but not the deep significance of a teaching—our lineage. Woolly Mammoth is reminding you that your relatives are calling you. They ask that you acknowledge and join them to stand in a circle of many generations. What was then is now. Here, your ancestors will embrace you. Eventually, you will have to say your farewells knowing that one day you will join them. Even though your ancestors dwell in another dimension, they are with you because they left you their lineage.

We all want to be remembered. Follow the custom of visiting the burial sites of your dead relatives. Spend reverential time there. Leave a little pinch of tobacco or other small gifts. Leave your prayer ties in a tree near their grave. Sacrifice to the ancestors by burning sage, copal or some other incense. If this is not possible, build an ancestral altar in your home and do rituals to their memory. Traditionally, these altars are built in the west.

Call out to the ancient ones. Let them energize and protect you. The trumpeting Woolly Mammoth brings you strength from the ancestors. She can grant any wish, so if your question is about a hope, expect a positive outcome. Woolly Mammoth rests in the shade of the ascending tree. The sacred tree of life holds the blooms of the precious ones. You can find nourishing fullness in the shadow of this ancestral tree.

In a time long past, the people uncovered bones of incredible length and diameter buried in the earth. The people knew these remains belonged to a creature of massive proportions that had walked the land in the days of the ancestors. This place of discovery was called "where-they-are-broad-shouldered." Withdrawn from the earth, the bones were honored in a sacred space and revered as being the testimony of giants who came before us.

Woolly Mammoth Card evokes ancestral protection for the less able who are weakened in mind, body or spirit—and need to be held in a supportive realm so they can develop. Woolly Mammoth can discern the spiritual family you belong to and the practices that will be most conducive to your spiritual growth. The prehistoric creature reveals ways for you and your descendants to be strong and healthy as you move into the future.

You may feel unfamiliar with the spirit world. But all around us are gifts from the past—buildings, inventions, philosophies, and the nomenclature of life as we know it in modern times. Let these manifestations speak to your consciousness. Experience and reason form only a small part of our perceptions of reality. The card suggests you can learn to communicate with your ancestors. Open yourself to the daily signs and occurrences that hold deeper meaning for you.

Press on with your life but remember your origins. Walk the spiral road to the bridge of the old souls—your ancestors. Go in spirit to where they live amidst the pebbly stars. By using intuition, divination, prayer and other methods, we can catch that sacred blast from the past.

This is Woolly Mammoth's teaching.

RED PARROT
Hearing

Red Parrot is associated with the number eleven, which the Mayans represented with two horizontal bars with a single dot above. Each horizontal bar, like the rung of a ladder, is a new level of reality, a new world. The dot is the seed, sown in the ground of the new world, containing the spark of all its potential.

At noon, the spirit of Sun Face, the fire, the Red Parrot would come sweeping down from the sky to rekindle the sacrificial flames.

Red Parrot, like the scarlet macaw, is considered precious, and is also associated with hearing. Red Parrots travel in pairs and are called Sacred Red Twins, guardians of the red echo. Sound, a gift from the ether, seeds our world.

Red Parrot reminds us that there can be no sound without silence. There is a fracturing of the celestial harmonies and the manner and form in which we hear. Red Parrot, with fire and hearing medicines, teaches us to listen carefully, so that we might hear original music, the sound that carries the name of the Holy One.

Red Parrot Woman prophesied to the people in olden times. She was a tiny native woman in a red hat and red coat. She was holy. Once two Red Parrots came to the village square and began to make a loud squawking. The people got fed up with the noise and threw stones at them. But still, the birds didn't budge, squawking louder day and night. The wise elders went to the birds and asked what they wanted to tell them. The elders could not understand the squawks of the Red Parrots. People had lost their ability to communicate with other forms of life.

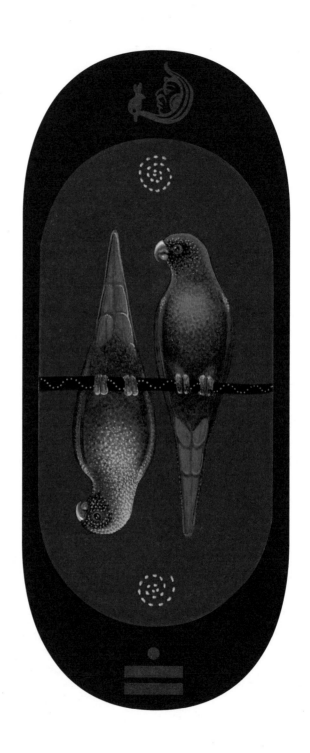

Now there were at this time holy twins named Lizard and Magpie. The twins lived in a grove of trees outside the village with their father. The twins talked with trees. They talked to stones. They even talked to the wind. The people deeply respected and acknowledged these powers of the twins. The elders went to the twins' father and asked if the twins would come and tell them what the Red Parrots wanted.

The father agreed to this. Magpie and Lizard were taken before the Red Parrots. The twin children squawked and the Red Parrots squawked back for a long time. Then the twins informed the people that the birds predicted the coming of a violent people in wind-driven canoes. This tribe would be dressed in metal garments. They would ride on the backs of enormous dogs. They would bring unknown diseases with no cures, wars, destruction, misuse of sacred tobacco and other sacred plants and animals, new gods, and eventually, there would be death-bringing monsters made of metal appearing on the earth and in the sky. There would be no way to prevent these things from happening. Sadly, the minds of the people were closed to prophecies. They could not hear and comprehend the words the twins spoke. Years later, the people were completely unprepared for the arrival of the ferocious men dressed in metal.

Red Parrot is associated with the ears. These birds have developed superb powers of hearing and are able to mimic the slightest nuance of human language. Red Parrot has the ability to hear sounds from a great distance. Red Parrots are the keepers of the powers of clairaudience. The ancients knew how to use this ability.

Red Parrot has the ability to project sound that can clearly be heard at a long distance. Oddly enough, this power dwells behind the bird's eyelids. Red Parrot can pinpoint the exact meaning of any spoken word by listening to the sound inside the sound. Red Parrot's teachings make it possible to hear and become a channel for spirits existing on other planes. Red Parrot feathers are bound with rain and sun. Red Parrot's feathers are used in music-making to conjure the intricate red rainbow of sound. Red Parrot instructs us to always hear what is being said. Deep inside the great silence there is a song from your "self" to your "self." The sound is quick and delicate. The inner-you calls within the deep stillness. And the inner you hears the call and understands the oneness of all creation.

T
H
I
R
T
E
E
N

C
O
U
N
T

C
A
R
D
S

Red Parrot Card is telling you that you are not listening, or you are listening to the wrong stuff. You aren't hearing beyond your own noise. Listen. Listen well. Tune in and hear deeply the sounds generated by the world—wind, rain, sirens, traffic, human and animal language. Listen to the insect musicians playing and singing their unearthly chorale. Listen to the beat and rhythms of life—the poetry of simple sound.

"Really listen up," is Red Parrot's message, "for there is an answer waiting for you." You might be sitting in a café or enjoying yourself at a party, and you overhear precisely the information you need. If you have ears, make Red Parrot happy and use them. Your inner voice may tell you where to find a new friend or make connection with an old one. The answer to a haunting question you have been struggling with is near. "I told you, but you didn't listen to me," squawks Red Parrot.

The noise and sound pollution in the world today lead us to tune out. Red Parrot Card asks, "Are there too many voices bombarding you? Be selective. Embrace life and drop the illusory." Choose carefully what you listen to and turn off the noisemakers. Learn to listen with discernment. Red Parrot Card reminds us, as sons and daughters of the humming Earth, to turn to the heavens and listen. The answers to our current dilemmas cascade down from the great silence. Listen, listen, Red Parrot says. Listen and you may truly know what the galactic wind is saying. You may even hear the Voice of Voices.

SCORPION
Retribution

Beware. Scorpion throws curves in a major scale. The signature of twelve symbolizes cosmic winds and the laws of celestial symmetry. Twelve is the lost wisdom number of mystical emanations and is the twelfth fluctuation, which can break patterns within oscillations. The Western world plays the number twelve by doing the solar dozens with their calendar months.

Education in the ancient societies was open to girls and boys of all classes. However, the training was so demanding very few became priests or priestesses. The combination of vigorous physical challenges and the intellectual capacity required of the mystical brother- and sisterhoods were met by only a handful of highly disciplined individuals.

Children beginning at the temple schools were faced with depravation and even death. They slept on reed mats on stone floors. They subsisted on gruel and water. They were sent forth to gather up venomous scorpions that skittered through the night shadows. If a child was stung, he or she suffered terribly and rarely survived. Upon recovery, whatever the outcome, the child was dismissed from the temple school. Only those children with the dexterity, temerity and smarts to capture the scorpions night after night were initiated to the next level.

Hereafter, they were given the wisdom of the cosmos as they were trained in sacred mathematics, astronomy and ceremony. They were taught the languages of animals, the jaguar, the eagle and the great horned owl. They were readied to hold the interface between heaven

and earth. No longer simply human, they offered their intellect and physical being to the great round of activity that kept the planet in right relation to the Sun, Moon, Venus and all inhabitants of our galaxy.

The temple priests and priestesses coated themselves with black body paint containing scorched scorpions. This paste had a psychotropic ingredient that opened doors to other worlds, which ceremonial leaders could enter. As the sacred calendar was set forth with a ceremony every twenty days, constant fasting, auto-sacrifice, dreaming, prognostication and calculation was required on the part of temple technicians.

One of the most rigorous cycles required the temple leader to pierce his tongue with sharp sticks the size of an index finger. The blood was caught and offered in supplication; the cycle of sacrifice, purification and regeneration was repeated endlessly at the temple.

All this activity was overseen by the black God M, the Star Scorpion. His tail was the terrible black sacrificial knife constantly drilling for fire. It is said that there is a wheel of sorrow and retribution. In life, we walk the way of good and evil. The wheel turns in endless cycles of learning life's lessons. Some people trip, lose their balance, and fall into suffering and pain. They encounter brutality and ignorance. These are the helldivers that have stumbled on hatred, greed and enmity.

Watch your step! Scorpion smiles and waits for you at the end of Pebbly River, the Milky Way Galaxy. The eye of the Scorpion is a cruel one. In this mirror-eye we clearly see our unbalanced judgments and insatiable drive for power over others. We seek to punish those we imagine have wounded us. Retribution is a vial of spiritual poison distilled from the blossoms of hatred and fear. The flowering of this evil plant is often rooted in injustice and ego distortion. It can cause sickness and feelings of inadequacy and distress. It is a garden sown with the bitter weeds of jealousy and anger.

Pregnant women once wore the tattooed image of the scorpion over their navels because of its life-bridging power. It was a call to the pathway of stars to send a healthy spirit to the fetus. Scorpion is the hinge that swings open the door of life and death, offering protection or assault. Here choices are weighed. This portal is a difficult passageway to enter.

Scorpion is saying don't look outside. Misfortune, causality and acts of another do not exist in the nest of the Scorpion. You receive according to what you do. Scorpion presents us a gift for changing our restricted point of view so that we can again harmonize with the subtle music of the spheres.

Scorpion instructs us to pay attention to our activities and involvements. Beware of too much passion. Beware of vices and the consequent humiliation when you fall prey to them. Be wary of impure thoughts or intense feelings that may lead to poor judgment. You may find yourself in the land of hungry ghosts, the dimension of greed, selfishness, addiction and insatiable lust.

Scorpion teaches many lessons. Scorpion gives an opportunity to learn from painful mistakes. The sting of Scorpion ends our complacency immediately. We scream and curse our predicament. Wisdom is born from it. Scorpion teaches us to laugh and cry in full measure. She often brings a sting to our ego and our ignorance, and in this destructive act she creates anew. Scorpion teases with her poisoned scimitar. She will sting herself to death rather than surrender to any power. Call on Scorpion and always fight for your right to be. She dances a dance of no return and instructs us that we do the same.

Scorpion is a guardian of farmers and gardeners. She tells you to prepare the ground and plant your garden. Scorpion advises you not to lie and strictly honor your word. Examine contracts carefully before signing. Scorpion Card can give you beneficial advice on health issues. You may have to visit the family hearth and do some politicking.

Scorpion dances the cosmic dance just as the Sun and stars dance. The Earth is a dancing dervish whirling in space. We human beings dance a sacred dance inside the hallowed circle of eternity. We are all artisans of the dance and the ceremony of life. Remember you may not be responsible for the tune but you are certainly responsible for your own choreography. Learn from Scorpion.

Dance your dance with consciousness and passion.

TOBACCO
Truth

Thirteen is the numinous heart of sacred geometry and is a number that has great importance in ancient astrology and prognostication. The number thirteen represents the highest heaven. Even though our search takes us in many directions, this heaven we seek is within, and the way there is Truth.

The guardian of the Tobacco plant is the tobacco caterpillar from whom you must ask permission to gather ritual Tobacco. Hummingbird's favorite nectar is from the Tobacco flower. This bloom is often used for ritual smoke, purification and to call the rain during drought. Tobacco grows at the entrance of many worlds. Sacred smoke can carry you safely into these unknown territories.

Tobacco was born from the Star Skirted One, known as the Milky Way containing the Galactic Tree. It came from the stars. Ancient priests and priestesses carried bottle gourds filled with tobacco tea. Tobacco was often mixed with powdered lime to increase its visionary qualities. It was smoked as cigarettes, cigars and in pipes. It was chewed to relieve fatigue and to slake hunger during fasts. This power plant linked worlds and it was, and still is, our most sacred relative.

Six-fingered silver giants came from the stars and were the first visitors to come to our planet. The six-fingered giants shone like brilliant mirrors. There has been much debate as to whether these giants were spirit or substance. Existence of the giants has never been questioned. The six-fingered beings walked about on the newly formed Earth blessing it, blessing the plants, animals and the people.

One day, the silver beings said they must return to the stars from whence they came. The people were very sad to hear of their imminent departure. A six-fingered silver being called forth the eldest woman in the village. The being said, "Reach inside of my chest and find my gift to you. It is a gift of my essence." So the old woman pulled out many tobacco plants and held them in her hands. The silver being instructed her on how to plant, harvest and prepare the plant in a sacred manner. "One day we will return. We will recognize you by visible essence, by your prayers and how you have kept this sacred gift from the stars." So it is told.

Ritual tobacco is often smoked at the base of a medicine tree. Tobacco holds the truth of all truths—our essence. Tobacco holds powers beyond anyone's comprehension. It is an offering and an intercessor to the spirit world. A puff of tobacco smoke can bring about a change in the entire universe. Proper use of Tobacco can foster wholeness. Tobacco reminds one that even a holy plant can be made profane. One must always relate to Tobacco in a respectful way because of its immense power.

The Tobacco Spirit instructs you to know your garden, and how it nurtures your body. Know your mental garden, the one that produces food for the mind. Be careful how you feed this garden so that you don't grow harmful thoughts. Know your spiritual garden and feed it with good spirit food. Tobacco has long been considered such a food. Even packaged up in corporate greed and sold by gaudy Madison Avenue hucksters, Tobacco is still holy. Never demonize any of the Plant Nations.

The keepers of this land called Turtle Island smoked sacred tobacco many thousands of years ago. It was smoked in reverence for ceremonies and rituals. The old ones had the vision to pray for the generations to come who would inhabit and take care of our mother. They prayed that future humanity would love and be responsible for all aspects of our sacred planet. They prayed for all the animals, trees, rivers, lakes and mountains. They prayed for the sky. They prayed for the elementals. They prayed for the spirit beings. They prayed for prosperity and peace for all humanity. They prayed for wisdom and understanding among all people. They prayed for future generations. They shared the sacred smoke and it winged upward, lifting to the Mysterious One.

Now those old prayers have been said. The old ones are gone. The knowledge of who they were is all but forgotten. They are the spirits that linger in power places. Their prayers are the reason we have such wondrous blessings. Those old ones see the world we have made and are crying for us in the spirit land.

T
O
B
A
C
C
O

Tobacco Card sends out the hope of a fearless spiritual life. It holds high ideals and asks you to live them. It asks you to pray for family, friends, clan and nation, and for all people. Pray for courage and honesty. Pray for the old and the young. Pray for all the animals, insects, and all water and water beings. Pray for the sun and the galaxies. Pray for our universe. Don't leave anything out intentionally. Tobacco tells us we are all in it together. We are all related.

145

L
A
D
Y

G
R
E
A
T

S
K
U
L
L

Z
E
R
O

146

LADY GREAT SKULL ZERO
Remembering

Seven holes there are
In the center of the world
In the sacred skull
Where all roads meet
At point zero

"It is complete. I am coming," says Lady Great Skull Zero. "The tied-up sun has set. The smoking stars are gathering. I am waiting for you at the end of night.

"It doesn't matter who you are—emperor, queen, pope or president—whether you are highborn or low. It doesn't matter what your religious convictions are or what god you worship. I am coming."

Yes, it all comes to zero.

Lady Great Skull Zero sits in the back of time. Life slips away through our fingers like ephemeral sand blowing away in the wind. The grains of sand were our actions while dwelling on this planet. Night and darkness and cold will come. But at the end of the long dark night, the light bursts forth. Life as we know it is darkness. And death, in its gorgeous simplicity, is all of the light from which we have been separated.

Lady Great Skull Zero, the Queen of Terror, symbolizes the necessity of death. Death comes in many guises. We may undergo many ego deaths in a lifetime. Hidden inside these ego deaths is liberation, a transition to what we truly are. You watch your possessions or your ideas and talents stripped away to lie at the feet of another. You see your gifts misunderstood and misrepresented by charlatans and liars. Friends or lovers disillusion you. No matter how painful death is, you can congratulate yourself when you experience the little death, the death of the ego, a birthday gift from Lady Great Skull Zero.

Naked truth is death and there is only this to remember. It is not easy in sanitized modern cultures to gaze upon Lady Great Skull Zero. However, various religious teachings tell us to meditate on death. See where it takes you. Learning of death and dying puts one on a road of appreciation and deeper meaning.

A circle of thirteen macaws preen their feathers and strut around the fallen bones that surround Lady Great Skull Zero. Pyre and tombstone are her amulets. Lady Great Skull Zero calls silently from the tomb. "All that is beautiful will one day be gone. Drink your fill of life, for soon you must come to me."

Lady Great Skull Zero is motionless, without desire, actionless and free. She is able to process the fear around any situation or question. When you can remember, you remember who you are. Then you know there is nothing to worry about.

Lady Great Skull's teachings are manifold. She represents the void and eternity. Zero is nothing. She is the keeper of the invisible and yet all is born from her. She may simply be telling you to rid yourself of the past or some other good riddance. Lady Great Skull Zero can free our intelligence. The skull is the House of Mind. It is the part of the body most resistant to decay. The top of the skull touches the vault of heaven and it is the zero point between hell and heaven. Remembering is not in the memory. True remembering arises when we are pristine and beyond delusion. All the energies come to rest in a moment and we are suddenly free.

Lady Great Skull Zero Card asks you to analyze what is dead in your life and release it. Death and resurrection were at the center of the people's lives in ancient times. The cycle was played out every day in the exalted and mundane. For example, the people witnessed rebirth in the pathway of Venus, the drama of the ball courts and even in the corn they ate each day. Venus was the brilliant morning star who died and was reborn as the mysterious and dangerous evening star. The people witnessed the play of cosmic destruction and recreation at the ball games. Maize sacrificed and died so that humans could grow flesh.

Tie the fragments of your life together in such a sacred and seamless expression. For Lady Great Skull Zero is a challenge card. Are you willing to step through your ossified behaviors into a larger perspective? Are you able to walk away from the familiar into the unfamiliar? Are you willing to surrender and clasp the bony fingers of Lady Great Skull Zero? She will take you to a place you always were and always will be.

THE CENOTE

Starlight strikes
The midnight pool
Turning, flickering
Swirling across Grandmother's eye.

Sacred Cenotes are naturally occurring wells and sources of fresh water. They are ceremonial sites and places of pilgrimage. Cenotes are deep sinkholes in the earth containing much power and revelatory potency. The Cenote is a circle of emptiness swirling in violet darkness. It is a deep basin containing running waters of jade. This ancient sacred space and the road leading to it were synchronized with the turning of the heavens and activated by ritual invocation and other ceremonial means.

The Cenote is simple but it contains an infinite source of knowledge. To have life on Earth, human souls have passed through the Cenote to this world in which we are now living. And as the teaching explains, we can return back through the Cenote to clairvoyance and relearn the meaning of our existence. One submerges in this holy portal and returns with answers.

The Cenote is a template that delineates an array of energies that influence and guide our action on the Earth plane. Cenote is the interface between Earth and Sky, and holds the moment the Sun aligns perfectly with Galactic Center in late December, 2012. It is the pool of the astromancer because the surface water of the Cenote unceasingly reflects the upper world, the night and day sky. Astronomy of our kinship with the cosmos is recorded in the inner universe of the Cenote. New light has been sent to the Cenote from a living and awakened dimension. This is the merging site of the fusion of possibility.

Cenote is the heart of the Oracle, the blanket of darkness. It is the obsidian night. It is the great black bowl containing the void. It is the other side of the light that envelops the hemisphere. It is the invincible darkness always there. Darkness permeating worlds. It is the inward repository of spirit—spirit pushing outward and made manifest. From darkness comes the restoration of light and from spirit comes matter. Four Jaguar spirits herald the approach of the New Humanity and guard the Cenote. The spirits keep watch from inter-cardinal points near the perimeter of the jade ring. The jade ring holds the cosmic energy of perfection on Earth, power, authority, truth and harmony. The Law of Jade is a celestial mandate from the highest order of the universe. The jade ring is a circle of ultimate purity.

The Jaguar Guardians are sentinels protecting the Jade Ring with a web of fibrous light energy. Used in ceremony or rites of passage, the Cenote Cloth can be very useful. It is an intersection of earth and sky and jaguars protect ceremony. Ceremonies and rites can be thought of as webs in this sense: if a ceremony is done correctly, it repeats the structures of the ritual into a larger web of being.

Emerald Jaguar, Gold Jaguar, Obsidian Jaguar and Turquoise Jaguar tirelessly observe the passing phenomenon within the Cenote—the heavens and the world below forming its imprint on consensus existence. Emerald Jaguar is the guardian of physical and spiritual transformation. Gold Jaguar brings healing forces of the forest into the Cenote. Obsidian Jaguar protects the Cenote from evil and from any negative psychic energy sent there by black magicians. Turquoise Jaguar brings harmony and unity to one's surroundings and in nonphysical realms. The Jaguar Guardians are the prophets bringing dimension and shape to the future. Prophecy explains that these holy Jaguars will usher in the next world, cast within the sacred Cenote dream.

Inscriptions on the Jade Ring reveal the Mayan numbers one through eight. Eight represents Venus. Nine is the interior number, hidden within the Cenote, and carries the essence of the Galactic Tree. There is a mathematical certainty to all substance. Numbers have esoteric meanings, which are jealously guarded by Mystery Schools. Numbers are the primary tool to establish cosmic location. Numbers used for counting time are different from those used in counting things or people. Each day of the old calendars made its unique harmony—its song within creation. Temporal form is alive with a multitude of qualities within the Cenote and holds a clear view of transitional states.

The Jade Ring protects elders and children. The Jade Ring represents zero and elders and children are the closest to the zero point after death / before birth. The Mayan glyph for zero is a clamshell. Zero is the mother number from which all numbers are derived. It represents eternity. Zero is nothing and contains the great silence. It is womb-like, feminine. The Jade Ring delineates the boundary of the Cenote. Cenote is the endless line of forever. A return is made to the beginning for the Jade Ring is a perfect figure. The Cenote concentrates energy and contains it.

One and two are to remind us of male and female powers and teach us of fragmentation. Three, four and five are related to the mind and show us that human mind is contained within the Great Mind. Six, seven and eight remind us of the directions and the elemental powers of fire, air, earth and water. These last three numbers, along with nine, contain all material form. Numbers from the Book of Fate, the holy number beings, nine to the transitioning zero, reside in the Cenote.

Cenote is one language for the wisdom of the sacred wheel and correlates with classic teachings. Inside the Jade Ring is the terminus for many unknown futures. The geomantic patterns of inner and outward circumstances can be divined. This territory configures many worlds and brings them into view. What seemed impenetrable is now received and understood.

The Cenote is a portal and one must open it and close it. The starry dynamics—the crystal-bead-necklace-above travels to the Cenote below and informs it. The Moon, the Sun and Venus are in the Cenote hidden. Cenote is a cosmic brain with Sun and Moon hemispheres. Put your questions, issues and problems in trust to the Cenote. Enter the magic of antiquity and learn to draw answers from this great well of celestial and earthly understanding.

CENOTE MOON

Black night, big face
Lop-eared rabbit
Engraved on a mica disk
Oh waining moon ~ moon
To the cenote going

Your gleaming rays
Melting strands of mist
Veiling the water lilies
In the blessing pool

Cenote Moon addresses our personal energies, the harmony and rhythm of our existence. Moon pours out her sacred, loving song. She sings to our soul so we can know our dance of being. Moontide memories are reawakened. She transmits to our blood our secret desires and passions. She phases our dark to meet our light. Humans must align with her cycles in order to find unity and peace.

Bring questions of harmony, happiness, inner strength and confidence to the Moon. Moon figures prominently in social activities and public affairs. The Moon is mental and the mind can be used as a weapon. If Moon disappeared, all mental activity would cease. Accordingly, she can be courted as an intellectual stimulus. She is an alchemist able to change things by reflecting upon them. Moon rules midwifery, mothers, mothering and motherhood.

For fifty thousand years, our various moons have been responsible for floods, earthquakes and global storms. Old stories tell of great turbulence in First Sky. For perhaps millions of years there was no

Moon. Then, various satellites were drawn into our orbit and revolved for thousands of years before crashing into Earth's surface. The capture of these moons, their approach and fixed collision has brought about cataclysmic change responsible for geological eras, biological transmutations, genetic mutation, and has enhanced the evolution of our species.

Moon is older than Earth which owes its being to Moon. Different Suns had different Moons. Our present Moon is the last of four previous moons. Our Moon was once a small planet with an irregular orbit around the Sun between Earth and Mars. A passing comet struck it. The little sphere was jarred and deflected from its orbital path. It became our Moon and began to circle earth about 13,000 years ago and set the cyclical conditions for new life and reharmonized culture. The Moon's patterning is reflected deep within us and she epitomizes the cyclic rhythms of life. Her magnetic power pulls on the seatides, our bodies and our brains. Moon influences rainfall and levels of water underneath the Earth. Twenty-eight is her sacred number and the number of a lunar month.

When the world was new and struggling to find its order, Sun challenged all the planets to a race to see who had the greatest endurance and who was the fastest. It was agreed that the Sun and all the planets would meet in a long valley. Eagle was chosen to be judge and time keeper.

Eagle told Rabbit about the event.

Rabbit became very agitated and said, "I'm a lot faster than any of them. It's no contest. I could beat them all with my eyes closed."

"Oh yes," said Eagle. "Remember what happened to you when you raced Deer?"

"Can't everyone forget that story? That happened a long time ago and I was a lot younger then. Now I'm older and much wiser. Believe me, if I race the Sun and the Planets, I won't stop and take a nap. I'll go the distance. Please ask Sun to let me race too."

"Well, okay," said Eagle. "I'll see what I can do."

Later, when Eagle told Sun about Rabbit's request, the Sun said,

"It will be another good lesson for Rabbit. Surely we are all much faster than him."

So it was agreed to let Rabbit enter the race.

The Sun, the Planets and Rabbit all lined up ready to run. Eagle let out a cry and they all took off. From the very beginning, Rabbit streaked out in front and led the pack. Sun lingered behind because he was exhausted from all his labors.

Seeing Rabbit far out ahead, Mars got angry and left the race early. Eagle disqualified him for threatening Rabbit's life. Jupiter was too fat, and could hardly breathe and so he dropped out. Mercury would slow down and then speed up losing ground each time. Saturn was disqualified for cheating because Eagle had caught her placing obstacles in the path of the runners so she was disqualified from the beginning.

Rabbit was first. Moon was right behind Rabbit. And then Venus was close behind Moon as they neared the finish line. Moon, with a spurt of energy and an intense effort, was right on top of Rabbit and appeared to be overtaking him. Unfortunately, she tripped. Moon fell right on top of Rabbit squashing him. Venus won the race and Moon got up and stumbled in last. Moon was never quite the same, according to this ancient astrological allegory. To this day, you can see Rabbit embedded on the face of the Moon.

Selecting an Oracle 2013 Card for the Moon position brings the reflected light of the moment into focus.

Moon is a passionate teacher. Ask Cenote Moon questions about family dynamics or dilemmas, dream meanings and personal growth. Ask Cenote Moon to reveal the mysterious powers of women and how to understand the many faces of women. Ask Cenote Moon about our dark inner-moon, which can pull us in deleterious ways. It can inspire strange longings to go forth on destructive roads.

Moon is Queen of the Night. She rules growth and many other hidden processes of nature. She rules hollow spaces of the Earth, movements of fluids and other elements within and upon Earth's surface. She draws the veiled potencies of stars and constelaetions to herself. She is able to receive and concentrate radiant emanations from other celestial bodies and filter and transmute them before pouring their bounty upon the Earth.

C
E
N
O
T
E

M
O
O
N

CENOTE SUN

Sunlight strikes
The midday pool
Blazing, blinding
Fording the dark pupil
A world afire
From above
One world from another.

Sun is our superstar.

The Earth moves on an elliptical orbit around the Sun. The speed of the Earth in its orbit is not a constant. The Earth speeds up and slows down as it swings around the Sun. Humanity has made time rigid and uniform through the technology of the clock. We measure time at a constant rate that is false to the rhythm of the Earth. The ancients experienced time as a variable that is closer to a genuine measure.

The ancient timekeepers synchronized heaven and earth. Life mirrored the patterns of the Sun, Moon and stars. It was a marriage between celestial order and the biological pulse of Earth. Generations of star watchers, moon watchers and sun watchers were greatly interested in the time between worlds, of creation and destruction—a calculation from present Sun to Sun's next manifestation.

Sun is the great white fire chief of the sky and is our principle light source. There have been many Suns, or ages. And every Sun has a story. Sun sings each new age into being. The Sun is now tuning its instruments and clearing its voice in order to sing another creation song.

Going down into the darkness and arising again in the day sky, Cenote Sun signifies the heart of life. The great warriors and women who have died in childbirth dwell in the House of the Sun. These spirits can be seen frolicking near the house and can be consulted for answers to many puzzling questions. Each day, Sun builds our house of enlightenment and Sun represents the supreme heights obtainable by our human family.

Sun is the divine potency. Life begins with a germinal Sun spark that brings life into being. Indeed, that radiation is life itself. Of course, all the various light virtues come into play. But a solar body exists within all sentient life. Simply put, we are all incarnations of the Sun.

The ancients knew this.

Sun is the battery that powers life. The Sun moves through stages of evolution. The Sun has a rhythmic pulse, a heartbeat. Accordingly, the Sun is moving into a tangible new state, hastening and unfolding each day. Ceremonial respect was shown to the Sun by ancient cultures because it was known that Sun figured prominently in one's health, prosperity, and the cure of physical infirmity. *Look to Sun to answer questions about a father or a husband.*

Sunrays are the outward manifestation of the source of our inner light. Sun is the furnace that heats the sacred fires of life. Cenote Sun is the subjective fire of our eye turned inward. Darkness and dangers disappear in its light. The Sun is at the center of our forehead. *Use the Sun to see the unseen.*

Sun is responsible for the celestial and geomagnetic mechanics of our entire solar field. Sun is our most prominent entity. It is the heart of our heavens blessing humankind with a continuous series of light. It is related to our own heart. The Sun's heartbeat is the sunspot cycle of twenty-two years, a very sacred number. Qualities of light from the Sun enhance life and Sun is the deep soul of our planet. The Sun is truthful and never lies.

It is the circle of molten splendor. It streams across our sky in blazing light. Sun is the effulgent eagle. There have been many Suns—world after world. Many more Suns are yet to come.

Cenote Sun addresses problems of wealth and finances, personal power, influence over others, and meetings with important officials or other authority figures. Since the Sun represents our body and the planetary system represents much of our bio-equipment, look to Sun to answer questions about health and energy. Ask the Sun to reveal the powers of men and how to understand the many faces of the masculine.

Cenote Sun is the great inner illuminator. It is our divine fire and we are made from this fire. Indeed, solar forces are contained in all matter. The Sun produces an essential energy. Humans, animals and all of life have this light quality in the very fabric of their being. We exist because of light. Humans have been compared to dancing solar holograms moving in a cosmic choreography mirrored to earth from our sacred Sun.

CENOTE VENUS

Then one inks the sky
With a silvery blast
A pink, blue, violet shiver
Dyes the sacred voyage
Over the watery eye of truth.

The light of Venus cracks the sky of our interior world. Venus is the plumed serpent. The ancients called this planet "oracle." The beloved Quetzalcoatl taught the people peace and love. He left on a spiritual pilgrimage and promised one day to return. He burst into flames and his heart of ashes rose up into the heavens and transformed into the planet Venus.

Within our planetary system, Venus is unique. The baked surface of Venus ripples with spidery forms—subsurface volcanic activity. It is a planet of fearful inconsistencies and contradictory influences. It is unconventional and can pull human life and human events in many directions. There is a strong connection between Earth and Venus. Yet the powers of Venus are little known in the western world.

Venus is unpredictable and dangerous, with the capability of emitting perilous rays. There appears to be a scientific correlation between Venus and flu outbreaks. This planet predicts periods of upheaval and social unrest. For this reason, the ancient astrologers created a table for tracking the syndical revolutions of Venus. Venus influences the deepest levels of human purpose. The lesson of Venus is the use of the human will to balance the intensity of light and darkness. This star's polarity must be handled with understanding and care.

In western European thought, Venus is associated with harmony and unity. Yet, for the ancient Americans, Venus was contrary to Earth. Contraries are holy, for they challenge us with the greatest of lessons. The contrary acts out an absurd wisdom on which we project our fears and fantasies. Venus transits our conscious and unconscious, our Sun and Moon. Venus, the diver, plunges deep into many worlds.

Venus has the lowest orbital eccentricity of all planets. Its distance from the Sun remains at 67,200,000 miles. Its axial rotation is locked to ours but its rotation is oppositional. European science began observing Venus transiting the Sun in 1631. The phenomenon of Venus transiting Sun has happened only seven times since then. The latest Venus transit was in 2004 and is slated to happen again in 2012. Venus transits happen in pairs separated by eight years and two days.

The contrary aspects of Venus test our spiritual aspirations time and time again. Sometimes, we are shocked and forced to look in horror at the human predicament. Other times, we feel the loving, soothing energy Venus can bring. Venus can place major impediments in our path or easily remove them.

Venus is our nearest neighbor planet, the second from the Sun and appears to us as the morning and evening twin star. Clearly, Venus projects a capricious and dangerous temperament. Tracing its trajectory in the morning or evening sky, it appears to jump. It weaves, dances and optically skips. For that reason it was often thought to be serpentine in nature. Venus lives deep in our dualistic nature.

The Morning Star, with her shifting degrees of radiance, with her curious violet glitter and diamond-like nature, was the good star, a messiah, teaching us the road of love and peace. In this aspect, Venus is the return of the plumed serpent, the Quetzalcoatl. Then Venus with another face appears. Venus, the Evening Star becomes visible, the *lus fero*–the Lucifer. This phenomenon of Venus Two Face has provided an ancient blueprint for the unfolding of many world religions.

The returning or New Sun predicts the coming of great movement. The ancients made careful calculations and forecast a cosmic reality check in 2012. The glyph *ollin*, earthquake or movement, symbolizes our transition. Our scientists measure the magnetic North and note that it is on the move at an average of ten kilometers per year.

Scientific studies of the mid-oceanic ridges reveal cyclical switches of the polarity of the Earth's magnetic field. Astronomers discovered the Milky Way also has a magnetic field in a corner of our galaxy we call the constelaetion Cygnus. This unimaginable dark mass is the sacred portal, the black band, the flowering ground of the starry ceiba tree, and the center of the Milky Way.

The mass at the center is three million times the size of the Sun and makes a complete revolution in eleven minutes. To put this in prospective, the Earth takes twenty-four hours and the Sun takes a month to complete a rotation. Clouds of dust and gas obscure this belt and make this dark energy difficult to observe.

Venus and Earth are aligned in a Venus-Sun transit during June of 2012. The ancient star watchers recorded that thirteen cycles of four hundred years would pass before their year zero would arrive. The year zero correlates to December 2012 when the sun aligns with the Galactic center.

Venus, the ancients tell us, ignited and hatched the light that produced life on Earth. Humankind, nature and the stars are inseparable. Venus embodies the necessary paradox to bind opposites. So with courage, we struggle to maintain balance within our own conflicted darkness and light. We choose. We seek to understand the powers of creativity and destruction and use them in an informed manner.

There is a story concerning Venus. At the time of this tale, near the very beginning, Venus was known as Dog of the Sun. There was only Sun and his dog, Venus, existing in the vast heavens. Working for the Sun was tiresome. Venus, Sun's dog servant, did as she was told and scurried about running the Sun's errands. The Dog of the Sun labored tirelessly each cosmic day.

After a long day of work, Sun yawned and went to bed for the night. Dog of the Sun curled up to sleep but hunger pangs prevented her slumber. Her bowl of food was empty. She paced the heavens. Her stomach howled. She howled, but the Sun was fast asleep. She sniffed around looking for a morsel of bone or meat. But there was nothing to be found.

Dog of the Sun whined and cried some more. Then she shook herself and trotted off into the great emptiness, into the cosmos— hunting for food. She tracked from side to side, zigzagging this way and that. She sniffed the void for signs. Now and again she whined from her consuming hunger pangs. Then, in the distance, Dog of the Sun saw a yellowish phosphorescent light and set off to see what it was.

She found an eerie village inhabited by monsters and giants. Their dwellings were made from mud and sticks and situated around a square. Dog of the Sun sniffed and sniffed, following her nose. Carefully, she sneaked around until she found a large pot behind the dwellings. Inside the pot was a kind of dried corn called hominy. Ravenously, Dog of the Sun began to gobble. Hearing the dog's loud chewing, a sleeping giant woke up, and went to investigate.

When the giant saw Dog of the Sun, he began beating her with a big digging stick. Dog of the Sun snatched a huge mouthful of the dried corn and she streaked across the sky scattering the kernels. Those kernels became the Milky Way Galaxy. It was Venus who created our Galactic Tree, so it is told.

Dog of the Sun, in just as many old tales, is son of the Sun or Son of the Father Sun. But mainly, in the oldest allegories, Venus was the awesome power of the feminine subverted to the patriarchy. The wholesome powers of woman will again cure the ills of a sick patriarchy, a design full of greed, cruelty, inhumanity, degradation, violence and continual war.

The planet Venus has many non-ordinary faces but *choice* is always her essence. Venus is the great star of magicians. But beware of the Venus of Backward Feet who can bring adversity and confusion. The white sky diamond can be beneficial or malefic, depending on which face she shows to Earth. Venus can be a menacing sky knife or arrowhead. With certain planetary configurations, Venus becomes a virtual blade pointed straight at Earth. Venus is the swordswoman cutting through our illusions.

Venus figures heavily in politics and political systems. Venus Eagle of Fire Darts and Venus of the Blazing Sword can bring social unrest and upheaval. Quetzalcoatl is linked to the rise and fall of civilizations and the return to order. Venus can cause great and sudden damage. But the abiding power of Venus can lead away from difficulty.

Venus is the most passionate of all planets. Let her answer questions about children and education. She may speak of comfort, opulence and beauty. She can answer questions concerning sexuality. She speaks of life and resurrection. Venus is truly the confounder, the precious paradox, the energy of the necessary opponent, and she can help us understand our own divided nature.

Venus has a binding energy, binding one thing with another. She attracts us with charm and seduction. She speaks a language of love, sex and the civilizing qualities of bonding and marriage. Therefore, look to this planet for suggestions on how to solve marital problems. Venus holds many clues about effective communication.

Venus often leads the Sun through the nine hells to new light. Ask Cenote Venus how to keep your heart free from jealousy and fear. Venus light can speed up regeneration or provide energy to heal wounds of the heart and spirit. Also, if you have a question about a personal war or conflict, ask Venus to help you draw up your battle plans. Then ask for help executing them.

Venus may be a messenger, the bearer of bad news. Rays from Venus predicted earthquake, volcanic eruptions and other great catastrophes such as war and famine. She also predicted times of plenty, peace and cooperation between people and nations.

Oral tradition has it that Venus is the home of the Little People who have come to Earth to either serve us or vex us. These little ones are ambiguous in nature. Little People inhabit caves and out-of-the-way places. These tiny beings have magical powers and transform into pure spirit. In fact, they are often described as the Venus Darts or the Seven Arrows, belonging to the Little People from above. These sky dwarfs appear in many guises all over the Earth.

Look to the little spirits around a problem or question. If you

CENOTE VENUS

*want to play with the powers of the Little People, you must study
and intuit the Venusian energies. Ask yourself, "What is it that
Venus wants to eat?" Venus is hungry for Solar, Lunar and
Earth energy. Feed Venus and in return expect a blessing from
the planet children of the Fourth Sky. The blessing of a powerful
Venus spirit can only enhance life in good ways.*

DOING AN OPENING RITUAL

The following are descriptions for opening rituals that can strengthen and enhance oracular skills. Be as simple or as elaborate as you desire. A prayer offered that the reading is successful is a powerful way to open. Light a white or yellow candle. Candles signify the old ritual of sacrifice. The first candles were made from animal fat—so a burning candle is an invocation for animal or other spirits to be present. Burn dried marigold, yarrow, sage, tobacco, sweetgrass, cedar, buck brush, copal or your favorite incense.

In contrast, you can evoke the spirit of Quetzalcoatl, the embodiment of the peaceful feathered serpent, who instructed the people to adorn their ceremonies with flowers and butterflies. Only pure beeswax candles were used when honoring the Flower Magicians. These candles are the antithesis of blood letting and animal or human sacrifice. The use of jade, turquoise, amber, pink seashells and abalone shells is appropriate. Use orchid or other flower essences. Flowers were revered over gold. Use prayer sticks, tobacco ties, or put a sage leaf in your pocket to bring purity to your prophetic powers. Color, flowers, beauty are all in the spirit of the beneficent ancient Mound Builders.

Make a boundary between your reading and the outside world. Make a sacred space set apart from everyday use. Cast a circle. A circle can be a whole, a hole, a nothing, a zero, emptiness and the womb of all being. If you have access to natural settings, you can do your readings on hilltops, open plains, among sacred tree growths, near springs, rivers or wells. Do them on mountaintops, by ancestral burial grounds or entrances to the underworld such as anthills or caves. All space is sacred. Readings can be done virtually anywhere.

As readers we are honor bound by the mysteries of the spirit to give clarity, encouragement, compassion and utter truth to the best of our ability. Divination is a responsibility. The reading process is no place to be manipulative, arrogant or flippant. Sitting before the Cenote one must be patient and humble until the mirror within signals in a cogent way.

THE SACRED MIRROR TWINS

When you use the 2013 Oracle Cards, remember it is an opportunity to enter sacred time and sacred space. The Cenote is an ancient map of connection and navigation through many combinations of patterns and structures of being. The map is not flat. It has within it an ancient energy—a deeper oracle that can be understood in countless concentrations of meaning. An Oracle reading is an initiation. The Cenote is a kind of sacred tipster. The celestial inner court of selected cards can advise you on the hidden order of events. With practice, revelatory power will improve. Study and application will increase your ability to discern specific meanings from the cards.

Many people already have a point of view about a question when they sit down for a reading. Often questions can be secondary. True, 2013 Oracle has the power to show us the unknown. But often the question becomes not a solution but a much more important question. The cards ask you to become aware and take responsibility for both problem and solution.

With the cards, you may reach a rich vein of creative challenge and possibility. Let their ancient voices give you permission to change your life for the better. The Oracle is not a strange and obscure way to divine the unknown. These cards aligned with their sacred purpose and powers can help you stop the roller coaster of the mind. There are many different roads to understanding. The Oracle offers an entrance to an ancient system of knowledge and the cards speak in many sacred languages.

There are no contrary or upside down positions for the 2013 Oracle Cards. The imagery of the cards is designed to supply the diviner with resonant forms. Each card can speak as an acutely sentient medium. For instance, the images on the Bee Card and Tobacco Card have optical effects. Touch one of these cards to the tip of your nose. Relax and let your eyes blur watching the images slide into each other. Slowly move the card about eight inches from the bridge of your nose. Rotate the card. At this point the right and left hemispheres of the brain are engaged, opening to different channels of insight.

By activating the delicate meta-imagery of various sacred geometrical configurations, the cards offer new dimensions of possibility that allow you to enter the symbol in a new way. One should approach the cards with clearness of intent. The more thoughtfully stated a question, the more powerful the transmission of revelatory power.

Reading the cards is a calling out to divine intelligence. To consult with the Oracle requires work, dedication and sensitivity. Spiritual effort sharpens awareness. For a simple reading, blow your breath on the black mirror surface on the back of the cards. Your first breath is a joining with creation and your individual spirit becomes the microcosm of the universe. Breath is sacred. Each precious breath you take is a complete life cycle containing all the aspects of your being. To blow your breath is to give a part of your spirit. As your breath settles on the card you may become aware of a sudden image or have a register of understanding. We breathe in. We breathe out our breathprint into unseen worlds, but the mirror catches it — a quick, subtle communication with ethereal possibility. Breath upon the mirror is a messenger. This is one of the earliest divinatory methods. Use breath readings alone or have those you are reading for blow their breath. This method is complete in itself but can also be used as a prelude to any 2013 Oracle spread.

Another simple reading begins by asking a relevant question. Remove the Zero card, and then divide the deck into two stacks putting the Thirteen Count Cards on the left and the Twenty Count Cards on the right. Shuffle each pile and take a random card from each using your left hand to select from the left pile and use your right hand to select from the right pile. Now hold the mirrored surface of the two cards in front of you without looking at their pictography. Play a little game with the mirrors. Send your face back and forth as if it were a batted ball in a game of mirrors.

Let the game stimulate your imagination as profoundly as in ancient times. Carried within your psyche is a memory of standing near a still pool and seeing yourself mirrored in the water—just as in the water of the Cenote. This experience taught the principle of the soul—of our deeper self being detached from our physical self. In fact, the energy of the human reflection in the water was believed to be the energy that separated from the body at death. It is a great mystery; catoptromancy, or mirror divination, has been done in one form or another since the dawn of human history.

Divine the mirror for omens. Meditate on it in relation to your problem or question. Ask the mirror to help you. See how the mirror gifts you. It takes practice but observe the mirror soul and let it lift you beyond your limitations. It can inspire you with unusual responses to your inquiries.

Consider that response. Then, turn the cards over to see what you have drawn. Let the cards further illuminate your inner understanding. Reach beyond cultural constructs to a deeper awareness. Use the Thirteen and Twenty Count cards as a guide and reference point. By using the 2013 Oracle Cards, one can enter a world of great antiquity and power. Each 2013 Oracle Card holds a description of ancient guidance. Interpreting the cards is not difficult. Find answers to your immediate problems. Use the 2013 Oracle Cards to help you meet new challenges. The lessons are ancient but more relevant today than ever.

THE CENOTE SPREAD

From the depths of the Cenote come answers. Sun sheds light and divinatory meaning. Moon and Venus, our closest cosmic family members, have potent predictive qualities. Within the Cenote walls of jade there is an ancient geomantic landscape—from the above to the below. 2013 Oracle Cards placed inside the Cenote circle can be marked, plumbed, balanced, simplified, explained, and made pertinent to our lives.

The Cenote is for readings concerning choices about transitioning to the next step of planetary evolution and traversing the complex changes of our times. With the use of the Cenote, the rational mind can be rendered secondary and deep consciousness becomes primary in the overall divinatory process. Like the oracles of old, we can dip into the well and drink from its mystical wisdom.

Cenote is a miraculous predictive mirror. In the past, there were many other kinds of mirrors that were used for divination. Reflections in a divinatory mirror can bring one to the simplest truth, a sudden signature of comprehension. Use the mirrors for a penetrating glance into the spirit—the place of causality where what is bound becomes manifest.

For a Cenote reading: Shuffle the 2013 Oracle cards together. Once you have asked your question, hold the cards for a few moments in order to establish a connection. When you are satisfied, fan out all the cards face down so that the plain black surfaces are showing. Draw one card at random and turn it over. Compare the card to the Key on the back of this book to find the page number that will identify it.

(If you first select the lady Great Skull Zero card, you have come to a place before measure, where a new distrubution of energy can emerge. Place lady Great Skull Zero in the middle of the cenote and draw three more cards to suggest how to change the energetics of your life.)

If the first card drawn is a Thirteen count card with a moon glyph, the first card is placed on Cenote Moon and the reading for the three cards moves counterclockwise: the second card is placed on Cenote Venus and the third selected card is placed on Cenote Sun.

The first card always determines the orbit of the cards within the Cenote and the direction the cards are read inside the jade ring. Thus, if a Twenty Count card is drawn first, place it on Cenote Sun. Place the next card on Cenote Venus and the third card on Cenote Moon. The direction of the orbit of the cards cues the reader to the dominant energy of the reading. The Oracle addresses various divinatory levels enabling one to move through inflexible situations.

Look at these cards and their placement. As we sit before the cards, we are able to view ourselves from different perspectives. Think of these cards as benevolent teachers, learned oracles, ancient advisors. The images are sacred mirrors—mirrors that help us to explore a deeper truth. Think of these cards as shadows on the wall. Think of them as a sphere where future events may be seen with clarity depending on the powers you bring to the divining process.

Study the cards before you turn them over. The reflective surface of the mirror provides you with a tool that can be used with every reading. Mirrors have many teachings. Modern physics has studied the phenomena of light waves and informs us that the reflection one regards in the mirror is nanoseconds younger than the person viewing her or his own image. The eyes as the organs of sight can never help us see our true self. Just as it is impossible to stand in the same waters of a rushing stream twice, it is impossible to affix one's self to the surface of the mirror.

The Cenote becomes a mental dance ground, a space filled with a vital charge, a place where one confronts consensus reality and the spirit world. Dance yourself into the song of the New Creation. Meditate on the mirrors of your spread. Divination yields information that is hidden from worldly view. By focusing on a looking glass, so to speak, we activate the power to interpret the cards with strength and clarity of vision. Reflection is the mind turned inward upon itself. Deep within your mind is the answer to the question. You may be surprised to see that answer suddenly staring back at you.

During your meditation, look at yourself and examine your role within the question posed by the reading. Remind yourself to quit pointing away from your own truth. The mirrors ask you, "Who are you as a reader?" Are you the trickster, the healer, the warrior, the judge, the ruler, a pillar of strength or a saboteur? Are you a problem solver creating the bridge to a solution? Stop your critical mind. Drop all self-judgment. Become centered and open to an answer. Bring yourself into the moment. Let the past go. Let it be swallowed by pools of liquid obsidian. Bring your attention to the reading. Become co-creator with the present, moving toward a future of perfect choice.

The reading of the cards may be done in tiers. Three cards are selected and placed on top of the glyphs and divined. Again, if Lady Zero is drawn first, she goes in the center of the Cenote and you draw three more cards. The answer may be so obvious there is no need to consult more cards. However, if further clarification is sought, repeat the process. Each new tier begins with the selection of a card and is moved accordingly, either counterclockwise or clockwise. The second set of three cards is placed with mirrored faces showing over the first three cards. The last set of three cards is placed on the former set. The Cenote reading uses up to nine cards to be read in sets of three.

The mirrors are divined before the images. One reflects when doing divination. Ancient people always consulted the clairvoyant mirror. The Oracle influences human history—even to this day.

FOUR OTHER ORACLE SPREADS

The following four card spreads have been designed to answer different types of inquiries made to the 2013 Oracle. The configurations are based on visionary and cosmic solutions found by the temple mound builders. The four spreads are the Pathway of the Flower Spread, the Black Cosmic Cross Spread, and two Serpent Spreads – the Light Serpent Going To The Sky Spread and the Diving Serpent Spread.

Use these spreads to divine direction. Use the spreads to untangle conflicting and confusing thoughts. Unmask the hidden face of a question. Lift the veil in order to see the face of truth. Claim all-seeing jade eyes. Walk the black band to the mouth of transformation. See into the Cenote depths. Find out what you must do. If need be, you can first drop all guilt and shame into the sacred Cenote waters and be cleansed. Deck yourself with quetzal feathers and multicolored flowers. Give yourself permission to be powerful. Be strong. Meet your problems on the road and defeat them—one, two, three.

THE BLACK COSMIC CROSS SPREAD

The black timber crosses
On the star-strewn roads
Beyond our starcloud memories.

In the night sky
Carried on spinning cosmic winds
Dressed in the white skirt
Between stars she weaves
The black sash
Binding creations.

Physicists call it the black hole. Potent emanations of energy are emitted from this place of most dense matter. To the ancients it was the dark portal—the cosmogenesis of the voidlight that cradles our existence. Dust particles and gasses from our galaxy obscure this black wombcore that is the shape of an elongated cross. Our Sun and Earth will align with this core during the winter solstice of 2012. The cosmic womb of our galaxy will birth a New Sun.

So say the prophecies.

Powerful and simple in its geometry, the spread should be used only when a situation is in gridlock. One has come to an impasse. First examine the original intentions, cease opposing the situation and submit to it. Ask for help from cosmic intelligence. When there is seemingly no other direction to go, walk the black matrix binding the Galactic Tree. Two principles from alchemy are employed in this dynamic. First, you create a field of experience by engaging the present and the future. Secondly, you move events forward and backwards in time. By engaging these principles, you can move a seemingly irreconcilable situation forward. Entering the realm of divination, a supernatural light is shed upon the circumstances—the connection of the visible with the invisible.

Use only three cards. The first two cards should be placed on a south-north axis. The first card drawn is placed in the south and the second is placed in the north. The cards should fan out like the mirrored wings of a bird. The crossing card lies vertically between the two horizontal cards—the body of a bird flying upwards. This crossing card can be intuitively tilted during the reading—either left or right. Left is the recipient. Right is benefactor.

First, divine the mirrored faces, then turn the first card over, the second and the third.

Use the following card interpretations for this reading.

PRESENT CHALLENGES, CARD ONE

This card represents the challenge before you and hidden or overt powers working against you. This could mean your own unconscious or concealed enemies. There may be cultural, ethnic or gender bias directed against you. Examine all constrictions. Are there dark controlling magical forces afoot? Have you withdrawn into a shell? Where is the paralysis? This card presents a chance to do the introspection that was not possible as the current situation was materializing.

FUTURE CHALLENGES, CARD TWO

Use this card to see any future circumstances that impact the question. Where is the situation leading? What is the likely outcome if nothing is done? Define the oppositional forces in play. Mine the lessons. Once you comprehend with the mirrors of your mind you can glimpse the remedies available to you.

THE CROSSING-CARD, CARD THREE

The crossing card falls on the pivot point. Here the question is weighed and balanced on a fulcrum, the tilting black beam of the dark cosmic cross. Fulcrum is a lever that can move energy. Use it to reestablish positive momentum. The more serious the question the easier it is to balance. Can the question be weighted right or left? How do you transform the situation and achieve balance—a trans-situational equilibrium? Where is the positive within the question and where is the negative? Where is the polarity?

This crossing card may portend events beyond one's capacity to change. If this is so, one must adapt and find ways to accept reality. This card can aid one in adjusting. A retreat is frequently an advance—to let go is to expand. Find the hidden point of alchemical change. Look for the singular opportunity to favorably alter the course of events.

Problems have various magnitudes. There are physical, emotional and spiritual aspects to most questions. This card suggests solutions to one or more aspects of the situation. This divination is a dialogue with the numinous world. The galactic scale engages the present and future to convert strife into cooperation. This card spread seeks to create a state where minds are complementary. Minds are separated but connected by the balancing bar of our greatest scale uniting truth and wisdom.

The ancients knew justice cannot be fathomed through the eyes. Justice can only be divined. What falls from this divination comes into being.

PATHWAY OF THE FLOWER SPREAD

The Pathway of the Flower Spread is the spirit of hummingbird, bee and butterfly—the sweet road, the good road of beauty and light. Divine this path for unity of heart and mind. The Pathway of Flowers is the perfumed way that leads to spiritual purpose. Use it to find your soul's direction to fulfillment.

We search for the *rosa mystica*—the infinite glory of immaculate love. Flower is a symbol for beauty and victory. Consider the beautiful flower—how it elevates the spirit. What joy to the heart are these gorgeous flowers of many colors. Some flowers are visionary. Some are medicine flowers. All flowers have magical qualities.

There are four cards in the Pathway of Flowers Spread. The first is the Stem Card. The second is the Pistil or Seed Card. The third is the Stamen or Pollen Card. And the fourth card is the Petal or Blossom Card. These cards represent the entire flower.

Flowers are sacred—more precious than gold, so the ancients tell us.

THE READING

Select the first card as the Stem. The Stem Card leads upward to a row of three cards. The second card, the Pistil or Seed, is placed to the left. The third card, the Stamen or Pollen, is placed above the stem. The fourth card, the Petal or Blossom, is placed on the right. The entire card constelaetion represents the integrated flower.

The four cards have the following meanings:

FIRST CARD, THE STEM POSITION

The Stem of the flower represents the spine, the starting point for the path of energy. This card speaks of the personal journey towards fulfillment. This card describes your spiritual connection of Earth, matter. The Stem position addresses the foundation of your question. Keep in mind the first stages of the problem posed. How has it evolved to its present state? The seer should be able to detect the strengths and weaknesses within the query by divining this card position. What facet of the card's character is cast upon the Stem position? The stem of the flower counsels you to grow slowly. A network of roots hidden beneath the earth must develop to support the organism above. This card challenges you to visualize leafing and flowering from the depths of your soul.

SECOND CARD, PISTIL OR SEED POSITION

Find good loam, the rich fructifying loam of the Black House belonging to the Earth. Sow the seeds of a good medicine future. The minerals and vitamins and radiation of the Sun support and nurture the flower's growth. What elements support the life you are growing? What supplements should be added? Look to this card to provide the answer. Where are you planting your seeds and what sort of harvest will you reap?

THIRD CARD, THE STAMEN OR POLLEN POSITION

Pollen card is a means to bless yourself and others. Traditionally, pollen is offered to the Sun and holds the power to bless. The Flower Path Way is marked with Pollen and if you walk this road with integrity you will always know what lies ahead. Pollen represents the knowledge of eternal life. When you count your blessings and bless others, you are led to clarity of heart, mind and vision. In turn, you can take action in a manner germane to the unique situation. Help yourself and help others. Bring forth the beauty from within to manifest change in the world. See the beauty of all that you touch. *The Pollen position expands your awareness of the blessings, gifts and strengths that belong to you.*

Walk the Pollen Road to the blessed and the beautiful.

FOURTH CARD, THE BLOSSOM OR PETAL POSITION

How can one look deeply into a flower blossom and not be inspired by the beauty and utility of its design? The flower appears to have awakened for the benefit of all. For us, the flower has unmatched purity. Intuitively, we surround ourselves with blossoms when we want to evoke a pristine spiritual state. Our hearts burst open. We bloom. We live more naturally with kindness and compassion.

Flowers are great medicine teachers. Flowers offer us the chemical compounds to open visionary doorways. Flowers heal our bodies. They comfort and soothe our spirits. The Pathway of the Flower can take you to realms you never dreamed of visiting. The Blossom position guides us into life's profligate backyard. There, in a perfumed garden, the magical flowers are waiting. It is for you to let your best qualities come into flower and color the world by your presence.

The bee is drawn to the flower—the strong, sweet perfume from the blossoms. The Blossom position shows the way to spiritual fulfillment. With your flower eyes to guide you, you can recognize spiritual allies with a discerning heart. Consider working with an array of botanical essences and incorporating them into your daily routine. This card advises you how to flower and bloom.

SERPENT SPREADS

The following spreads are based on serpentine energy that was translated into light by the builders of the great Venus-enhanced temples. The temple astronomers observed Venus, the light giver, as this venerated planet appeared in a 260-day cycle. Venus was a celestial twin, a snake, a living presence at the forefront of consciousness. The ancients realized that Venus gave birth to the human race. They watched Venus and charted its course, day after day, without fail.

From these and other astronomical observations, very precise calendars were created which the people used as templates to maintain harmony between heaven and earth. One well-known Venus calendar was said to have begun in August 3114 B.C. Venus was known to have different aspects that influenced people's lives. Venus had many faces and personalities, some of which were beloved. Other faces were greatly alarming, so much so that people hid indoors rather than confront the fearsome Venus darts.

The people made great processions on the white road. They walked through sacred complexes, traveling to the holy Cenote. They made sacrifices to the spirit keepers of the water. Then they formed a human chain to represent the great undulating serpent and returned to the temple. The temple was a holy mountain. Over time, the temple mound accumulated spiritual serpent power and became the repository of ever-greater sacred energy. Up and down the face of the temple on the stairways, this energy poured. The great temples became spiritual batteries.

The Light Serpent Going to the Sky and **The Diving Serpent** card spreads activate the sacred technology of the temple mound stairway. The serpent pulse is a magical construct that manifests the power and authority of Venus and its divinatory qualities. Venus traces a five-pointed star, or pentagram, described by the elliptic path it takes every eight years. Our ancestors were profoundly inspired by the relationship they observed between Venus and Earth.

The spiraling Lord of Dawn, the divine twin, rolled and tumbled, changed and changed again. Once Venus changed into a fanged rattlesnake. So did the Lord of Dark Flint. The two serpents pulled at the corners of the void in order to give it a sacred geometry of dimensionality and form. Within their creation, animals, humans and other living beings evolved. This work made room for all upon the mother planet.

The Serpent Going To The Sky Spread represents the shadow snake leaping from earth to sky. The Diving Serpent Spread is based on the solar serpent. Each year at the spring equinox, sunlight hits the edges of the temple stairway. The undulation of light and shadow combine to form a massive kinetic rattlesnake. This represents the returning and the departing spirit of Quetzalcoatl. To the Cenote the spiritsnake returns. From the Cenote the spirit of the snakebird goes back to the Sky World.

There are seven temple steps in both the Light and Dark Serpent Spreads. All seven steps are important on the Serpent's Path. The steps have spiritual and physical implications. The temple stairway is an interactive and flowing system. Select and place seven cards on the right to represent the temple steps going up, and place seven cards on the left to represent the temple steps going down.

Think of each step, either up or down, as an interval of change. Consider each step as a way to navigate through the situation. Think of each serpent spread reading as the inner-sun on a journey of spiritual renewal.

Begin preparing the space in which you will do these two readings by placing a small bowl of water at the foot of the temple stairway. The bowl is symbolic of the sacred Cenote. Many startling forms may appear in this bowl and further illuminate the reading. After the cards have been divined and the reading closed, use the water in some resourceful way such as giving it to a plant or another body of water.

The Light Serpent Going to the Sky
Inner light and inner wisdom.

Ah, listen, my lord, my lady
Obsidian knife water
When you are cut,
Cut with the red blade
To free you and the light of you.
To go there, on the Serpent's Path,
Surging through the dimensions of this world.
She to the he. He to the she.
She to the three to the he.

Coiling, striking,
Go there to the breath of worlds
To the sound of the conch
To the sacred song
To the breath of him to her
Taking the Serpent's way up
Twisting, looping,
To the brazen urn of hearts
To sacred forfeiture
And essence carried to the jaguar sun.

The way of the serpent is the Venus way—the wisdom way leading to the inner and outer jaguar suns of enlightenment. It is the prophetic way, the vision and seeing way, the synchronistic way—the way of ultimate understanding. This spread represents the Quetzal Serpent climbing the holy mountain and flying into the great light. The step from the ground to stairway signifies the entrance from one world to another.

Step One, the Foundation Step: Examine the card and take the first ascending step. Two giant snails, one red and the other blue, are guardians of ascension. Red Snail represents matter. Blue

Snail represents spirit. A step taken between them represents the intertwining of physical and spiritual worlds. The two snails sense you with quivering antennae. Caught between cascades of yes's and no's, you can now see and understand in a more enlightened manner.

The act of climbing the First Step represents your commitment to engaging and transmuting the situation. This step begins with the questioner questioning the question. Within every question is an answer and within every answer is a deeper question. Make a simple statement of your intention thereby initiating magical principles. By focusing and releasing conflicting thought forms and emotions, the Venus energy can enthuse and lift you upward to triumph.

Step Two, the Star-strewn Step: Venus of the Star Link, high priestess, stands before her altar. Constelaetions move and dance across her black-mirrored eyes as she looks at you impassively. Her face is gray with sky-blue scales covering her prominent cheekbones. The crystal skeleton of a rattlesnake is draped from her crown. The clothes she wears are diamond-patterned and her bare arms are tattooed. She lives simultaneously in the human and cosmic worlds.

Venus of the Star Link challenges you to take the measure of your mind. Here the intellect is mirrored enabling one to investigate one's mental clarity. Here you consult with the high priestess and let her powers bless and transform the situation. Handing you the ritual flint knife, she instructs you to cut away the delusions that make you suffer. The flint dagger symbolizes a keen intellect married to noble truth. It denotes a rational examination of the question being asked. Bring knowledge and wisdom to bear on the problem or situation. Try to reduce facts into manageable increments in order to further dissect and analyze them.

Step Three, the Temporal Step: Examine the card for the Third Step upward. Encounter a raffish fellow, Venus with a bundle of time slung over his shoulder. His ear lobes are plugged with cut jade stones. Tattoos run the entire length of his body. His bundle holds fifty-two years as lived on the planet Earth. He is said to have a mind that is preoccupied with numbers, formulas and timekeeping. As you approach, he throws his arms open wide, showering you in the purest silver starlight, proclaiming you to be a being of eternal light.

Venus of the Bundle holds the mysteries of time in the Spirit Land of the Feathered Serpent. This holy place is not of this world, but within. As you begin the journey of ascension, you must take stock of what you have stored psychically within yourself. What serves you, and what patterns don't work and should be abandoned? How would you diagnose the health of your emotional realm? Does the personality you inhabit get the results you seek? Do you feel all parts of your person are unified? Can you sense a coherent wholeness where each aspect of yourself contributes to a totality that communicates you as an eternal light being?

If you feel life's journey lacks coherence and does not reflect your sacred vision, look to this card to restore order and sanity. Analyze the detours and byways you have taken. Why have you devoted so much precious time to these insignificant activities? What lesson is your soul trying to learn or avoid? Venus of the Bundle can assist you in defining the next step. Plot your course for completion of your aspirations.

Step Four, the Cultivation Step: Examine the fourth card. Venus of the Fields is grinding amaranth seeds at her stone. She heaps mounds of maize, beans, peanuts, squash, cacao and chili at your feet and declares it time for a feast. She scatters dried beans and aligns them in rows of thirteen by twenty to divine the correct course of action. The numbers 13 x 20 represent truth and humanity. Each day has a specific divinatory meaning such as dog, alligator, or monkey. Some days are weak and some are strong with life and possibility. How the day is fed speaks volumes about the future. This method of divination says to feed your days with the good food of a life well spent. Venus reminds you it is always harvest time somewhere on our abundant planet.

Our home is a garden and a matrix for a new world. Venus of the Fields charges you to reevaluate the yield of your harvest. She gives permission to abandon fields that aren't producing. Let the old fields lay fallow and reconstitute. As time unspools towards 2012, you will cut fresh furrows for new seedbeds. Venus recognizes a flowering, innovative, pioneering and wildly creative spirit. Nurture yourself and claim the spirit food offered by your environment.

Step Five, Step of the Flowering Way: Examine the fifth card. Astride the fifth step is Venus of the flower shield, ready to do combat. Unlike other soldiers, the Quetzal Butterfly Warrior wears no armor and carries no weapons. He is seen as vulnerable and unguarded. Quetzal Butterfly Venus embodies the alignment of thought and action. He views life with an eye that weighs everything equally. Quetzal Butterfly Venus sees himself in all things. Release all ideas of reward or punishment, gain or loss. This card suggests how to struggle against adversarial powers. One may learn to live by the heart and by this act, overcome barriers. The heart is a hunter hunting for completion and this step can help you find the way there. Fight for your rights. Do not be disrespectful but stand up for yourself. This card tells you how to struggle without losing the kindheartedness that animates you.

Step Six, the Step of the Vision Serpent: Examine the sixth card. Here stands Venus crowned with water-snake bird feathers and draped in a golden spotted coat. She is Venus of the Mind Flowers. Her companions are toads, who hop around her sandaled feet. She teaches the path of the Flower Weavers, the way of mercy and redemption. She prepares herself for sacrifice. When she cuts her flesh, flowers flow from the wound. She does this for the people. She anoints herself in wild lily and tobacco flower water. She may use orchid water or other kinds of water—sarsaparilla, sunflower or squash blossom.

Look to this card to discern how to bring peace and balance into the situation. What are the steps necessary to experience harmony? Let Venus of the Mind Flowers widen your perception and suggest ways to shape a solution for the problem or dilemma. This step enlists the dual powers of our deepest, most ancient unconscious mind and the helper spirits of flora. Become super-conscious and summon the harmonies of the flowers to aid in the resolution of any difficulty.

Step Seven, Eagle Plume Rising Step: On the Seventh Step, his torment and suffering finished, Venus with his Heart of Ashes rises to the morning star, completing his soul's pilgrimage. The sun swallows him. He is the Venus perfected. "Heed my words," he says. "I am become the divine serpent." Illuminated, he beckons from the sacred sky that we should follow without fear. Venus of the Heart of Ashes counsels to leave your earthly fears at the top of the temple mound. The seventh card suggests a means by which to transform your fear. This is a message to cast away your concerns and fly upward into the realm of the New Humanity.

The Diving Serpent Spread
Devours problems to release one from suffering.

He had taken so many by the hand and led them
To the House of Pure Light
To the great renewal,
To the blazing mirrors.

The light-bearing Eagle shrieks,
Calling the visionary star,
Sends her snaking downward.
She to the sacred palisade
She to the temple top.

Lord and Lady,
You with honor, tradition and blood
A falling reptile
Full of silence and grace
On the downward path
Of the pulsing heart.
Descending
To thread the deft weave
Of existence.

Venus, with the face of the diver bee, reconfigures and becomes the dark serpent diving downward from the Milky Way into the heart of the *anima mundi*. His jaws open to devour human folly and ignorance. Venus, the feathered serpent, beckons us to follow the serpent path of knowledge, wisdom and release from suffering.

Falling, falling, the spirit plunges through star-clouds. Blindness and then sight, inertia and vitality. Corruption and purity, no form to form. The rope uncoils from the galactic tree. The strands untangle as you fall backwards. Descend to earth, to the House of Magic. You fly, you fly, like the magicians of old.

Select seven cards. Begin at the top of the temple and place a card to represent each of the pyramid steps. The pinnacle of the temple is animated by substance joining with spirit.

Step One, Pinnacle Step: Take the First Step down. Encounter Venus of the Double Faces who casts a double shadow. Walk between the Mirrored Twins, morning star and evening star. Walk between male and female. Walk between shadow and light. Dig for the paradox inherent in you question or situation. How does it feel? Where is it in your body? Consider the locus of the question you have evoked. Where do you hold it? You would have greater freedom and power if you would clear this energy. Grapple with the illusion of gain and loss. Remove the resistance and become a vessel for healthy resolution.

Step Two, the Painted Step: Venus, in a skirt of red and black feathers, is on the third step. Venus, with his eyes of rainwater, stands waiting. These visionary eyes can move you through fog-smoked vapors, and his gleaming eyes of rainwater mirror your own eyes. This step represents the opening of the magical eye body.

Acknowledge the healing intelligence of water. Each raindrop is a prism holding rainbows. Paint your world with washes of color to evoke the changes you want. Bathe in blessed rainwater. Remake the imagery that enlivens you. Examine this card to foresee how this can be done.

Open fully to the House of Color. Explore the deeper meanings of your question by seeing it in a New Light. What color is the question or dilemma? What are the colors in your life generally? What colors are swirling into your life from outside sources? Does your being emanate a loving spectrum of color?

Step Three, the Passage Obscura Step: On the second step down, meet with the cloud-adorned Venus—the Venus of Mists, good woman sent from above. This wise and holy woman is covered with quaking, swirling eagle down. She steers the seeker through the obscured terrain—great guiding mistress of dimensions. Remember, your soul dropped from starry heights. You incarnated and you are learning. Reclaim self-knowledge, self-sufficiency, self-reliance and self-respect. Venus of Mists has made herself visible to you.

Ask her to navigate you through spiritual issues. Where is the spirit moving through the question? Let the focus be on sacredness. To see the holy mountain, we must let the mists clear. This takes time. When viewed from eternity, emerging answers take on a remarkable simplicity. The dullest question becomes a bright light because every act has a spiritual significance. Venus of the Mists reminds us to touch the clouds and bring spirit into the present. Use her as a guide in all that you do. If you can find the soul of a question within the obscuring mists, you have come a long way toward determining the answer.

Step Four, the Step of Decision: On the Fourth Step, Venus is clad in jaguar skins, he of the holy mountain. His headdress is crowned with blue-green hummingbird feathers. His mouth holds teeth of jade. This is the Venus of many prophetic visions. His scepter represents the visionary ruler. In days of old, rulers made the greatest sacrifices. Extreme sacrifice was a requirement of their office.

Here is a chance to establish a visionary connection and dialogue with your sacred inner authority figure. Listen to a higher intelligence within yourself. The hummingbird hovers near, fearless and aggressive. Let the hummingbird pierce your heart, propelling you through self-created obstacles. Center your consciousness in the center of your chest. Let it burst open like a flower while looking at your dilemma

THE DIVINING SERPENT SPREAD

in a simple, loving way. Open to divinatory gifts. Select and choose effective actions to take. A decision must be made before you leave this step.

Step Five, the Step of Passion: On the Fifth Step is lovely Venus, the blue-winged spirit of pollen and flower. In her right hand, she holds the hive. In her left hand, she holds the honeycomb. She dances the dimensions, choreographing steps in sun-drenched splendor. When she flies through the air, her rattle buzzes. A train of bees follows her. She brings the muses so that you may undertake any creative project.

Sweetness of language issuing from your golden mouth is a gift from the blue-winged Venus. She advises you to find the magnetic path, work hard and be sensible. If inclined, become involved in community affairs; perhaps work with a group of people to express your higher ideals. Speak with carefully considered words. Blue-winged Venus counsels you to become aware of your inner sweetness.

Step Six, the Step of Fear: On the Sixth Step towers the masked Turquoise Venus of the white fang. Your fear, negative thoughts, and personal failures are food for his terrifying Venus mouth. Let the mouth consume your pain of loss, separation, abandonment or grief from ancestral fate. Regroup, pray, meditate and focus on workable solutions to your difficulties. Have the courage to let go of concepts that no longer serve any good purpose. This card suggests ways to eliminate all unnecessary attachments.

Step Seven, the Step of the Precious Unity: This last step brings a new beginning on the earthly plane. Take the Seventh Step and walk barefoot on the welcoming earth to the flowering tree. The guardian of the Ceiba Tree is the sparkling dew-dressed Venus. Acknowledge her by embracing life. Touch the tree trunk and look upward to the four branches that form the cosmic cross. The four petals of the white blossoms are the sacred offerings of the holy tree. You are perfect, like the tree, and need no spiritual trappings or material possessions. Your soul is omnipresent. You stand beneath the flowering tree in immaculate beauty.

Long ago, all the gods and goddesses prepared for the first sundance. They readied the dance grounds of the void. They raised the great tree of the Milky Way Galaxy. Our star, the Sun, was a brilliant flower on that tree. Within you is that holy star and it will shine forever.

THE DIVING SERPENT SPREAD

ABOUT THE AUTHORS

David Carson was born and raised in Oklahoma and has long been immersed in the spiritual and prophetic aspects of the ancient Indigenous legacies of the Americas. A novelist who has written prolifically for newspapers, films and social reform publications, he is author of the memoir *Crossing Into Medicine Country* and coauthor of the best-selling *Medicine Cards, The Discovery of Power through the Ways of Animals*. He has lectured and given animal consultations and card readings to thousands of people worldwide to guide them to their personal truth and he has worked with Aztec and other shamans from as far away as Siberia and Hawaii.

Nina Sammons has a background in documentary filmmaking and creative writing, and has contributed articles to many magazines. She is a founding member of the *Taos Review*, a New Mexico poetry and literary publication. She lives in Santa Fe, New Mexico, with her twin daughters and husband.

Illustrator **Gigi Borri** lives near Parma, Italy. His work is in galleries and collections in Europe and the US. He is an author of *Anime Della Foresta, Tracce di un Mondo Sciamanico*. He is an expert in jungle plant and animal shamanism. He was adopted into a tribe in Indonesia and feels a deep kinship with his people. He learned firsthand of the powers of the jaguar while living in the jungles of South America. Borri is an impeccable ceremonialist and has participated in sundances and other rites.